Musical Architecture Secrets: Structure Planning For Guitar Composition

University Scholastic Press

UNIVERSITY SCHOLASTIC PRESS
New York   London   Rome

Other Musician's Series Books
By University Scholastic Press:

A Guitarist's Grimoire: Unlocking the Secrets of Creating A Musical Diary To Master Guitar Composition

Storytelling With Sound: Fundamentals of Creative Guitar Composition

Musical Architecture Secrets: Structure Planning For Guitar Composition

Strings Of Brilliance: Mastering Melody and Harmony Development For Guitar Composition

Rhythm Mastery for Guitarists: Unlocking Tempo and Timing Techniques For Guitar Composition

Table Of Contents

Introduction 9

Clarify Your Vision..13
   Defining Emotional and Thematic Essence................................13

Inspiration And Structure 17
   Analyze Other Musicians..17

Intuition And Structure 22
   Experimentation Using Intuition 22

Structure Planning...27
   Mapping Out Song Structure..27
   General Song Structure Template...27
   Additional Considerations..30

Common Song Structures..31
   Understanding Common Song Structures 31

Mood and Dynamics...34
   Considering Mood and Dynamics...34

Genre Structures 38
   Exploring Genre-Based Structures 38
   Rock..38
   Blues 39
   Metal...40
   Pop...41
   Jazz...41
   Folk..42
   Country 43

Blend Structures 44
   Creating Hybrid Structures 44

Modal or Freeform Structures..48
   Characteristics of Modal or Freeform Structures.....................48
   How to Create Modal or Freeform Structures.........................49

Riff-Based Structure..52
   Characteristics of Riff-Based Structure 52
   How to Create a Riff-Based Structure for Guitar Composition........53

Narrative Arc...56
   Structuring and Narrative Arc 56
   Define the Narrative Theme 56

Instrumentation And Structure...60
   Instrumentation Strategies 60

Transitions And Structure 64

Playing Style And Structure 68
  Assessing Playing Style And Strength 68

Revision And Structure 73
  Openness To Revision 73

Determine Section Lengths 77
  Consideration of Length 77

Conventions and Structure 81
  Align with Songwriting Conventions 81

Verse-Chorus Structure 85
  Explore Verse-Chorus Structure 85

AABA Structure 89
  Exploring ABBA Structure 89
  How to Create an AABA Structure 91

ABAB Structure 93
  ABAB Structure Overview 93
  How to Create an ABAB Structure for Guitar Composition 95

Section Lengths 97
  Experimenting With Section Lengths 97

Chorus Impact And Length 101
  Emphasize Chorus Impact 101

Dynamics and Section Length 105
  Contribution of Dynamics To Section Length 105

Lyric And Melodic Content And Section Length 109
  Influence of Lyrical And Melodic Content 109

Energy Levels And Section Length 113
  Determining Desired Energy Flow 113

Song Narrative And Section Length 118
  Serving The Song's Narrative 118

Dynamic Contrast And Section Length 122
  Using Dynamic Contrast Between Sections 122

Repetition And Section Length 126
  Experimenting With Repetition 126

Instrumental Sections And Length 130
  Determining Length Of Instrumentals 130

Transitions And Section Length 134
  Achieving Effective Transitions 134

Audience Attention And Length 138
  Assessing Audience Attention Spans According To Genre 138
  Considerations for Gauging Attention Span 141

Building Confidence 143
   Trust Your Instincts 143

Dynamics And Song Structure 148
   The Role Of Dynamics 148

The Dynamic Blueprint 152
   Considerations For A Dynamic Blueprint 152

Dynamic Blueprint Outline 156
   The DYNAMIC BLUEPRINT OUTLINE 156
   Remember For Your Dynamic Blueprint 159

Gradual Buildups And Structure 160
   Utilizing Gradual Buildups In Composition 160

Contrasts And Structure 164
   Creating Contrasts Between Sections 164
   Creating Contrast Within Sections 168

Crescendos And Decrescendos 173
   Incorporating Crescendos and Decrescendos 173

Articulation Techniques 177
   Articulation And Dynamic Expression 177

Dynamics And Melodic Phrasing 182
   Experimenting With Tempo Changes 182

Contrast Between Instruments 186
   Create Dynamic Contrast Between Instruments....186

Instrumental Techniques And Dynamics 190
   Utilizing Dynamics On Instrumental Techniques 190

Muted Strums And Picking Patterns 194
   Experimenting With Strums And Picking 194

Silence And Pauses 198
   Leveraging Silence And Pauses 198

Dynamics And Lyric Emphasis 202
   Aligning Dynamics with Lyric Emphasis 202

Swells And Fades 206
   Effective Use Of Swells And Fades 206

Tone Changes 210
   Being Mindful Of Tonal Changes 210

Record And Listen Actively 214
   How To Listen Actively To Recordings 214

Considering Audience Experience 219
   Dynamics And Audience Experience 219

Feedback 223
   Sharing Your Composition 223

Intensity And Restraint..227
    Balance Intensity and Restraint 227

Closing 233

Thank You...236

Other Books 237

Index..238

INTRODUCTION

Welcome to *Musical Architecture Secrets: Structure Planning For Guitar Composition*, a definitive guide to unlocking the hidden mysteries behind crafting captivating and cohesive musical compositions on the guitar. In the pages that follow, you will embark on a transformative journey through the intricate world of structure planning, learning the essential principles and techniques that will empower you to create compositions that resonate deeply with your audience.

Just as an architect carefully plans and designs the blueprint for a building, a composer must meticulously map out the structural framework of a musical composition. This process of structure planning lays the foundation upon which melodies, harmonies, and rhythms can intertwine to form a harmonious and coherent whole. Whether you're a seasoned guitarist seeking to refine your compositional skills or a novice musician eager to explore the art of songcraft, this book will serve as your indispensable guide to mastering the art of musical architecture.

Our journey begins with the crucial step of **Clarifying Your Vision**. Before embarking on any creative endeavor, it is essential to have a clear understanding of the artistic vision you wish to express. Through exercises and reflection prompts, you will learn how to articulate your musical goals, identify your unique creative voice, and envision the emotional landscape of your compositions.

From there, we will delve into the intricate relationship between **Inspiration and Structure**. Drawing inspiration from a myriad of sources, we will explore how to channel that creative energy into coherent musical structures that captivate the listener's imagination. You will discover how to find inspiration in the world around you, draw from diverse musical genres, and infuse your compositions with meaning and depth.

As we continue our exploration, we will tap into the power of **Intuition and Structure**. Guided by your innate musical instincts, you will learn to navigate the creative process with confidence and conviction. Through hands-on exercises and real-world examples, you will discover how to trust your intuition, make bold creative choices, and craft compositions that resonate authentically with your audience.

With a solid foundation in place, we will dive into the heart of our exploration: **Structure Planning**. Here, you will learn the essential principles and techniques for crafting effective musical structures that engage and captivate the listener. From analyzing **Common Song Structures** to exploring specialized forms such as **Modal or Freeform Structures** and **Riff-Based Structures**, you will gain a comprehensive understanding of the architectural blueprints that underpin successful compositions.

Throughout our journey, we will explore a wide range of topics, from the role of **Mood and Dynamics** in shaping the emotional landscape of a composition to the impact of **Genre Structures** and **Blend Structures** on the overall sonic palette. We will delve into the intricacies of **Transitions and Section Lengths, Instrumentation and Structure**, and **Playing Style and Structure**, providing you with practical tools and strategies for sculpting your compositions with precision and finesse.

Join me as we embark on this enriching journey through the secrets of musical architecture. Together, we will unlock the hidden mysteries behind crafting compelling and cohesive compositions that leave a lasting impression on both performer and listener alike. Let the adventure begin!

Instrumental Structures:

Instrumental compositions may follow different structures, often allowing for extended solo sections.

Frequent use of repetitive motifs and evolving dynamics.

Example: *Cliffs of Dover* by Eric Johnson.

Remember, these structures are not strict rules but rather guidelines. Musicians often experiment with variations and combinations to create unique compositions. The key is to serve the song's emotional and narrative goals while keeping the listener engaged through thoughtful arrangement and progression.

CLARIFY YOUR VISION

Define the emotional and thematic essence of your composition. *What story or message do you want to convey?* Understanding your vision will guide your choice of structure.

DEFINING EMOTIONAL AND THEMATIC ESSENCE

Defining the emotional and thematic essence of your guitar composition is a crucial step in creating a compelling piece of music.

Ask yourself these questions:

What Emotion Am I Trying to Convey?

Consider the overall mood you want to express, such as joy, melancholy, excitement, or introspection.

Clarify by imagining the emotional response you want from the listener. How should they feel when experiencing your composition?

What Is the Core Theme or Message?

Identify the central idea or story you want to convey through your music.

Clarify by distilling your theme into a few keywords or a short sentence. This will help you stay focused on the core concept.

Who Is Your Audience?

Consider who you are creating the music for. Different audiences may connect with different emotions and themes.

Clarify by visualizing the ideal listener and thinking about what resonates with them emotionally.

Are There Specific Influences or Inspirations?

Reflect on any musical or non-musical influences that inspired your composition.

Clarify by making a list of these influences and analyzing how they contribute to the emotional and thematic elements of your piece.

How Do Different Sections Contribute to the Overall Theme?

Break down your composition into sections (verse, chorus, bridge) and analyze how each contributes to the emotional journey.

Clarify by ensuring that each section aligns with the overall theme and contributes to the emotional progression of the piece.

What Is the Relationship Between Melody and Harmony?

Explore how your melody and harmony choices enhance the emotional impact of your composition.

Clarify by experimenting with different melodic and harmonic elements to see how they affect the overall mood.

Is There Symbolism in Your Composition?

Consider whether there are musical motifs, rhythms, or specific chords that symbolize or represent elements of your theme.

Clarify by consciously incorporating these symbols throughout your composition for coherence.

How Do Dynamics and Tempo Contribute to Emotion?

Analyze how variations in dynamics (volume) and tempo influence the emotional intensity of your composition.

Clarify by experimenting with different dynamic and tempo changes to find the most effective emotional impact.

What Visual Imagery Does the Music Evoke?

Think about the visual images that come to mind when listening to your composition. How can you enhance these images?

Clarify by considering how elements like texture, articulation, and pacing contribute to the visual experience.

Implication for Song Structure: Collaborative playing allows you to leverage the strengths of other musicians. Design sections that showcase each member's abilities, creating a harmonious blend of musical elements.

Do I Prefer Linear or Non-Linear Song Structures?

Question: Am I more drawn to linear song structures (verse-chorus-bridge) or non-linear structures with unconventional arrangements?

Implication for Song Structure: Your preference for linear or non-linear structures will influence the overall organization of your composition. Explore ways to experiment with structure while maintaining coherence.

Reflecting on your playing style and strengths as a guitarist is a continual process that evolves over time. By asking these questions, you gain insights into your musical identity, allowing you to make informed decisions when shaping song structures. Ultimately, the goal is to leverage your strengths, preferences, and unique voice as a guitarist to create compositions that resonate authentically with both you and your audience.

INSPIRATION AND STRUCTURE

Draw inspiration from musicians and compositions you admire. Analyze how they use song structures to convey emotion and captivate the listener.

ANALYZE OTHER MUSICIANS

Analyzing other musicians to understand how they use song structures to convey emotion and captivate listeners is a valuable exercise for enhancing your own guitar composition skills.

The following are some more questions to reflect on to assist you in determining your own guitar composition structure.

How Do They Establish a Mood in the Introduction?

Question: How does the musician set the mood in the introduction of the song?

Implication for Guitar Composition: Understanding how artists establish a mood at the beginning of a song can inform your choices for creating impactful introductions in your own compositions.

What Role Does Dynamics Play in Conveying Emotion?

Question: How do dynamics change throughout the song, and how does this contribute to emotional expression?

Implication for Guitar Composition: Observing how musicians use dynamics can guide you in incorporating changes in volume and intensity to evoke emotions in different sections of your guitar composition.

How Do They Transition Between Sections?

Question: What techniques do they use to transition between verses, choruses, and other sections?

Implication for Guitar Composition: Studying transition techniques helps you develop seamless connections between different parts of your composition, contributing to a cohesive musical experience.

What Role Does Instrumentation Play in Conveying the Emotion of the Song?

Question: How does the instrumentation contribute to the emotional impact of the song?

Implication for Guitar Composition: Analyzing the role of different instruments, including the guitar, can inspire you to choose specific tones, textures, and techniques that enhance emotional expression in your own compositions.

How Do They Build and Release Tension?

Question: In what ways do they build tension, and how is it released within the song?

Implication for Guitar Composition: Learning how artists navigate tension and release informs your ability to create engaging and dynamic progressions in your guitar compositions.

What Strategies Do They Use for Climactic Moments?

Question: How do musicians build up to and handle climactic moments in their songs?

Implication for Guitar Composition: Analyzing climactic moments helps you understand how to structure your composition for maximum emotional impact, especially in sections like solos or powerful chord progressions.

How Do They Use Repetition for Emphasis?

Question: How do they employ repetition, and what effect does it have on the listener?

Implication for Guitar Composition: Studying how artists use repetition allows you to leverage this technique in your guitar compositions to emphasize key themes and enhance memorability.

How Does the Song Structure Support the Lyrics?

Question: How is the song structure aligned with the lyrical content, and how does this contribute to emotional resonance?

Implication for Guitar Composition: Aligning your guitar composition's structure with lyrical themes can enhance the overall emotional impact and narrative cohesion.

How Do They Create Diversity Within Sections?

Question: What strategies do they employ to create diversity within verses, choruses, and other sections?

Implication for Guitar Composition: Exploring how musicians introduce variety within sections inspires you to experiment with different guitar techniques, tones, and arrangements to keep your compositions engaging.

How Do They Conclude the Song?

Question: How do they conclude the song, and what emotions or impressions linger?

Implication for Guitar Composition: Studying how artists conclude their songs helps you think about effective ways to wrap up your guitar compositions, leaving a lasting impact on the listener.

What Role Does Silence Play in the Song?

Question: How do they use moments of silence or breaks, and what purpose does it serve?

Implication for Guitar Composition: Understanding the strategic use of silence can guide you in creating pauses or breaks within your guitar compositions for added emphasis or to create anticipation.

How Do They Navigate Instrumental Sections?

Question: In instrumental sections, how do they maintain interest and convey emotion without vocals?

Implication for Guitar Composition: Analyzing instrumental sections helps you explore techniques to keep your guitar compositions engaging, especially if they include extended solos or instrumental breaks.

Use Technology to Your Advantage:

Digital Workstations: If you're using digital audio workstations (DAWs), take advantage of their flexibility. Easily rearrange sections, experiment with different sounds, and iterate on your composition in a non-destructive manner.

Save Versions: Save different versions of your composition as you make changes. This allows you to revisit and compare variations, ensuring that you're making informed decisions during the revision process.

Trust Your Instincts:

Personal Connection: Trust your instincts and your personal connection to the music. If a particular revision resonates with you on a deeper level, it's likely to have a similar impact on your audience.

Iterative Refinement: Understand that each revision is an opportunity for iterative refinement. Your composition will evolve, and each iteration brings you closer to realizing your artistic vision.

Being open to revising your initial song structure is an integral part of the creative journey. It allows you to refine, experiment, and elevate your composition to its full potential. Embrace the collaborative process between your original inspiration and the evolving nature of your music, and you'll find that each revision brings you closer to creating a guitar composition that truly captivates and resonates with your audience.

INTUITION AND STRUCTURE

Ultimately, trust your intuition and experiment with different structures. The more you explore, the better you'll understand what resonates with your vision for the composition.

There's no one-size-fits-all approach, and the right song structure for your guitar composition is the one that best serves your artistic vision and communicates the intended emotions or story to your audience.

EXPERIMENTATION USING INTUITION

Experimenting and trusting your intuition are crucial aspects of the creative process in guitar composition. These elements allow you to break free from conventions, discover unique sounds, and infuse your compositions with a personal touch.

Create a Playful Environment:

Explore Without Judgment: Set aside any self-criticism and create an environment where experimentation is encouraged. Allow yourself to explore different ideas without worrying about perfection.

Play Freely: Approach your guitar with a sense of playfulness. Experimentation often leads to unexpected discoveries, and a playful mindset opens the door to creative exploration.

Try Unconventional Techniques:

Extended Techniques: Experiment with unconventional guitar techniques. This could include alternate tunings, percussive playing, tapping, or incorporating objects like slides, bows, or e-bows to create unique sounds.

Sound Exploration: Use your guitar as a sonic palette. Explore the full range of sounds it can produce, from gentle harmonics to aggressive distortion. This experimentation can add texture and character to your composition.

Play Outside Your Comfort Zone:

Genre Blending: Step outside your preferred genre or style. Fuse elements from different genres to create a hybrid sound. This cross-pollination can lead to fresh and innovative compositions.

Unusual Chord Progressions: Experiment with chord progressions that challenge traditional norms. Dissonance and unexpected harmonic choices can add intrigue and depth to your compositions.

Record and Reflect:

Capture Ideas: Record your experiments, whether through a simple audio recorder, a smartphone, or a digital audio workstation (DAW). This allows you to document ideas in real-time.

Reflect on Recordings: Listen back to your recordings with an open mind. Pay attention to elements that stand out or resonate with you. These recordings can serve as a reference for building upon promising ideas.

Trust Your Initial Instincts:

Immediate Reactions: Trust your immediate reactions to certain sounds or combinations. If something feels right or resonates with you, trust that intuition. Your initial instincts often lead to authentic and emotionally charged compositions.

Capture Spontaneity: Don't shy away from capturing spontaneous moments. These unfiltered expressions can become the core of your composition, adding authenticity and emotional depth.

Experiment with Song Structures:

Non-Traditional Structures: Challenge traditional song structures. Experiment with non-linear forms, unconventional verse-chorus arrangements, or explore modal and freeform structures. This can result in compositions that feel fresh and unpredictable.

Dynamic Shifts: Play with dynamic shifts within your composition. Experiment with sudden changes in intensity, tempo, or mood to create contrast and maintain the listener's interest.

Collaborate and Seek Feedback:

Collaborative Exploration: Collaborate with other musicians or seek input from peers. Their perspectives may introduce new ideas and approaches that you might not have considered.

Objective Feedback: Be open to constructive feedback. Others may notice elements that resonate or suggest improvements. Balancing your intuition with external perspectives can enhance your creative process.

Embrace Imperfection:

Imperfections as Character: Embrace imperfections as part of the character of your composition. These quirks and unique qualities can distinguish your work and contribute to its authenticity.

Non-Linear Growth: Recognize that growth as a musician and composer is often non-linear. Experimentation might lead to unexpected results, and perceived mistakes can become valuable learning experiences.

Balance Exploration and Structure:

Structured Chaos: Find a balance between exploration and structure. While experimentation is essential, having a foundational structure provides a framework for your ideas. Aim for a harmonious blend of spontaneity and organization.

Iterative Refinement: Allow your composition to evolve through iterative refinement. Experimentation doesn't end with the initial idea; it's an ongoing process of discovery and refinement.

Cultivate Patience and Persistence:

Patience in Exploration: Understand that not every experiment will yield immediate success. Be patient with the process, and recognize that some ideas may need time to develop.

Persistent Iteration: If an experiment doesn't produce the desired outcome initially, iterate persistently. Small adjustments and refinements can transform an idea into a compelling composition.

Consider the song *Little Wing* by Jimi Hendrix. The iconic guitar work in this composition showcases Hendrix's willingness to experiment with

STRUCTURE PLANNING

Choosing the right song structure is a crucial step in shaping the overall form and narrative of your guitar composition. The chosen structure provides a framework for your musical ideas and influences the flow of the piece.

MAPPING OUT SONG STRUCTURE

Before adding dynamic changes, have a clear understanding of your overall song structure.

Identify the sections (verse, chorus, bridge) and the emotional arc you want to create throughout the composition.

Creating a detailed song structure map for a guitar composition involves outlining the arrangement of various sections, transitions, and dynamics throughout the piece.

Below is a general template for a song structure map that you can adapt to fit your creative vision. Keep in mind that this is just one example, and the structure can vary based on your preferences and the genre of music you're working within.

GENERAL SONG STRUCTURE TEMPLATE

Introduction (0:00 – 0:15)
Description: Establish the mood and set the tone for the composition.
Elements:
Chord progression or riff
Atmospheric effects

Minimal instrumentation

Verse 1 (0:15 - 0:45)

Description: Introduce the first section of the song with lyrics or instrumental melodies.

Elements:

Guitar chords or arpeggios

Simple melody

Lyrics (if applicable)

Pre-Chorus (0:45 - 1:00)

Description: Build anticipation and transition into the chorus.

Elements:

Dynamic chord progression

Increase in intensity

Foreshadowing of the chorus melody

Chorus (1:00 - 1:30)

Description: Present a memorable and impactful section.

Elements:

Strong chord progression

Vocal harmonies (if applicable)

Full instrumentation

Verse 2 (1:30 - 2:00)

Description: Reintroduce the verse with variations to maintain interest.

Elements:

Similar to Verse 1 with subtle differences

Additional instrumentation or variation in chord voicings

Instrumental Break (2:00 – 2:30)

Description: Allow for instrumental expression without vocals.

Elements:

Guitar solo or instrumental section

Dynamic variations

Focus on the guitar's tonal qualities

Bridge (2:30 – 3:00)

Description: Provide a contrast to previous sections and build tension.

Elements:

Change in chord progression

Experiment with different time signatures or modal shifts

Introduce new melodic ideas

Chorus 2 (3:00 – 3:30)

Description: Revisit the chorus with added intensity or variation.

Elements:

Similar to the first chorus with added dynamics or instrumental layers

Vocal variation (if applicable)

Outro (3:30 – 4:00)

Description: Conclude the composition and create a sense of resolution.

Elements:

Wind down the intensity

Revisit elements from the introduction or verses for thematic closure

Gradual fade-out or definitive ending

ADDITIONAL CONSIDERATIONS

Dynamic Buildups and Drops:

Use dynamic changes to create peaks and valleys in intensity.

Transitions:

Ensure smooth transitions between sections for a cohesive flow.

Instrumentation Changes:

Experiment with different guitar sounds, effects, or techniques to add variety.

Lyric or Melodic Hooks:

Identify and emphasize key lyrical or melodic elements for memorable impact.

Repetition and Variation:

Balance repetition for familiarity with variation to keep the composition engaging.

Remember that this structure map is a starting point, and you should feel free to adjust it based on your creative instincts and the specific requirements of your composition. The key is to maintain a sense of balance, flow, and emotional resonance throughout the song.

COMMON SONG STRUCTURES

Familiarize yourself with common song structures like verse-chorus, AABA, ABAB, and others. Each structure has its own characteristics and is associated with different genres and emotions.

Creating a compelling guitar composition involves understanding common song structures, which serve as the blueprint for organizing musical ideas. While there are numerous variations, some structures are widely used in popular music.

UNDERSTANDING COMMON SONG STRUCTURES

Verse-Chorus-Verse-Chorus (V-C-V-C):

Verse: The narrative or story-telling section where lyrics often progress.

Chorus: The central theme or message of the song, usually more musically and lyrically intense than the verse.

Bridge (optional): A contrasting section that provides a break between repeated verses and choruses.

Example: Many pop and rock songs, such as *Hey Jude* by The Beatles.

Intro-Verse-Chorus-Verse-Chorus-Bridge-Chorus-Outro (I-V-C-V-C-B-C-O):

Intro: A section that precedes the main body of the song, setting the tone.

Verse and Chorus: Similar to the V-C-V-C structure.

Bridge: A distinctive section that contrasts with the rest of the song, building tension.

Outro: The conclusion of the song, often a repetition or variation of the intro or chorus.

Example: *Mr. Brightside* by The Killers.

A-B-A-B (Binary Form):

Section A: The first section, often a verse.

Section B: The second section, typically a chorus or contrasting melody.

Example: Classical compositions often use binary form, and some pop songs, like *Good Riddance (Time of Your Life)* by Green Day, exhibit a modified binary structure.

A-A-B-A (Ternary Form):

Section A: The initial theme.

Section B: A contrasting theme.

Return to A: A return to the initial theme, creating a sense of completion.

Example: *Ain't No Sunshine* by Bill Withers.

Riff-Based Structure:

Instead of relying on distinct sections, some compositions build around a recurring guitar riff.

The riff might be the central focus, with variations providing dynamic changes.

Example: *Iron Man* by Black Sabbath.

Does Your Composition Tell a Story?

Determine whether your composition follows a narrative structure or if it evokes a sense of storytelling.

Clarify by outlining the narrative arc and ensuring that your musical elements support the storytelling aspect.

Regularly revisiting these questions during the creative process can help you refine and clarify the emotional and thematic essence of your guitar composition. Don't be afraid to experiment, and trust your instincts as you shape your musical narrative.

MOOD AND DYNAMICS

Reflect on the mood and dynamics you want to express. Some structures are better suited for building tension and resolution, while others may emphasize repetition and familiarity.

CONSIDERING MOOD AND DYNAMICS

Considering the mood and dynamics in your guitar composition is crucial for conveying the intended emotional impact.

Explore these key considerations and techniques to help you express the desired mood through dynamic choices.

Define the Mood:

Before diving into dynamics, have a clear understanding of the mood you want to convey.
Is it joyful, melancholic, aggressive, soothing, or suspenseful? Knowing the mood will guide your dynamic decisions.

Dynamic Range:

The dynamic range refers to the contrast between the softest and loudest parts of your composition. Consider how wide or narrow you want this range to be. A broad dynamic range can create more dramatic and expressive moments.

Start with a Dynamic Plan:

Outline a dynamic plan for your composition. Determine which sections should be louder or softer. For example, choruses might be louder for added intensity, while verses might be softer for a more intimate feel.

Gradual Buildups and Releases:

Use gradual dynamic buildups and releases to add tension and resolution. A gentle increase in volume can create anticipation, while a sudden decrease can provide relief or emphasize a transition.

Explore Crescendos and Diminuendos:

Experiment with crescendos (gradual increase in volume) and diminuendos (gradual decrease in volume) to shape phrases and sections. These techniques can add dynamic contour and emotional depth.

Accentuate Key Moments:

Identify key moments in your composition, such as a powerful chord change, a poignant melody, or a climactic section. Use dynamic contrasts to accentuate these moments and make them more impactful.

Dynamic Punctuation:

Use dynamics to punctuate different sections or changes in your composition. For instance, a sudden dynamic shift can mark the beginning of a new section or highlight a musical climax.

Consider Articulation:

Articulation, including techniques like legato, staccato, and hammer-ons/pull-offs, can influence the perceived dynamics. Experiment with different articulations to enhance the expressiveness of your playing.

Balance with Other Instruments:

If your composition includes other instruments, consider how the dynamics of each instrument interact. Achieving a balanced dynamic mix is essential for a cohesive and impactful sound.

Explore Texture and Instrumentation:

Varying the texture and instrumentation can contribute to the overall mood. Consider how different guitar techniques, such as fingerpicking versus strumming, can influence the dynamics and mood of your composition.

Recording Techniques:

If you're recording your guitar composition, explore different microphone placements and recording techniques to capture the dynamics accurately. Adjustments in mic distance, placement, and room acoustics can impact the perceived dynamic range.

Embrace Silence:

Silence and pauses are powerful tools. Don't be afraid to incorporate moments of silence in your composition. The absence of sound can be as impactful as loud or expressive passages.

Nirvana's *Smells Like Teen Spirit* includes a distinctive instrumental bridge that links the energetic chorus and the quieter verse.

Electronic and Acoustic Blending:

Combine electronic and acoustic elements to create a hybrid sonic landscape. Radiohead's *Karma Police* seamlessly blends acoustic guitar with electronic effects, contributing to its unique atmosphere.

Storytelling Through Structure:

Structure your composition like a narrative, with different sections representing distinct chapters or scenes. This narrative approach can be heard in Pink Floyd's *Shine On You Crazy Diamond*, which unfolds like a musical story with interconnected sections.

Genre Fusion:

Fuse different genres within the composition, blending elements from rock, blues, jazz, or other styles. John Mayer's *Gravity* incorporates blues elements within a modern rock context, creating a genre-blending hybrid.

Creating a hybrid form by blending different chorus-verse structures in guitar composition requires a willingness to experiment, break conventions, and explore new possibilities. Drawing inspiration from diverse musical genres and incorporating various songwriting techniques can result in a composition that is both innovative and captivating.

GENRE STRUCTURES

Different genres often have conventions regarding song structures. Consider the expectations of your chosen genre while selecting a structure, and feel free to blend or modify as needed.

EXPLORING GENRE-BASED STRUCTURES

Different guitar composition genres come with their own set of conventions and expectations regarding song structures.

We do an exploration of some genres and their typical song structures for guitar compositions, along with examples. Remember, these are just guideposts.

ROCK

Conventions:

Verse-Chorus Structure: Most rock songs follow a verse-chorus-verse-chorus-bridge-chorus structure. This conventional format allows for catchy hooks and memorable choruses.

Bridge for Variation: The bridge often serves as a contrasting section, introducing new elements or themes.

Guitar Solos: Rock compositions frequently include guitar solos, often placed after the second or third chorus.

Examples:

Stairway to Heaven (**Led Zeppelin**): This classic rock epic features a gradual build, a diverse set of sections, and an iconic guitar solo.

Back in Black (**AC/DC**): AC/DC's straightforward rock anthem follows a traditional verse-chorus structure with a memorable guitar riff.

BLUES

Conventions:

12-Bar Blues Progression: Blues compositions often revolve around the 12-bar blues chord progression, providing a foundation for improvisation.

Call and Response: The call-and-response pattern, where a phrase is played and then answered, is a common feature.

Repetition for Emphasis: Blues relies on repetition for emphasis, with guitarists often repeating specific licks or phrases.

Examples:

Crossroads (**Robert Johnson**): An early blues standard, featuring the traditional 12-bar blues structure and influential guitar work.

Red House (**Jimi Hendrix**): Hendrix's bluesy ballad showcases expressive guitar playing within a blues framework.

METAL

Conventions:

Riff-Based Structures: Metal often relies on powerful guitar riffs as the driving force of compositions.

Complex Song Structures: Progressive and technical metal genres may incorporate complex song structures, featuring intricate arrangements and time signature changes.

Guitar Shredding: Virtuosic guitar solos, known as "shredding," are a common feature in metal compositions.

Examples:

Master of Puppets (**Metallica**): A classic metal track featuring heavy guitar riffs, dynamic changes, and a notable guitar solo.

Through the Fire and Flames (**DragonForce**): An example of power metal with fast tempos, intricate guitar work, and extensive solos.

POP

Conventions:

Verse-Chorus Structure: Pop songs often adhere to a simple and catchy verse-chorus-verse-chorus-bridge-chorus structure for broad appeal.

Catchy Hooks: Memorable guitar hooks and riffs contribute to the overall catchiness of the song.

Melodic Solos: Pop compositions may feature melodic guitar solos that complement the vocal melodies.

Examples:

Shape of You (**Ed Sheeran**): A contemporary pop hit with a straightforward verse-chorus structure and a catchy guitar riff.

Every Breath You Take (**The Police**): A classic pop song with a memorable guitar riff, following a verse-chorus-verse-chorus-bridge-chorus structure.

JAZZ

Conventions:

AABA Form: Jazz compositions often follow the AABA structure, with the A sections presenting the main theme and the B section (bridge) providing contrast.

Improvisation: Jazz guitarists frequently engage in improvisation, showcasing their skill and creativity.

Extended Chord Progressions: Jazz compositions may feature extended and complex chord progressions, allowing for harmonic exploration.

Examples

Autumn Leaves (**Johnny Mercer**): A jazz standard with an AABA structure and room for extensive improvisation.

So What (**Miles Davis**): An iconic jazz composition featuring modal improvisation and a distinctive bass line.

FOLK

Conventions:

Simple Song Structures: Folk compositions often feature simple structures, commonly using the verse-chorus format.

Acoustic Instruments: Acoustic guitars are central to folk compositions, often accompanied by other traditional instruments.

Storytelling Lyrics: Folk songs frequently tell stories through their lyrics, and the guitar complements the narrative.

Examples:

Blowin' in the Wind (**Bob Dylan**): A folk anthem with a straightforward structure and socially conscious lyrics.

The Times They Are a-Changin' (**Bob Dylan**): Another example of a folk song by Bob Dylan with a narrative structure and acoustic guitar accompaniment.

experimenting with different picking styles, using effects pedals, or incorporating unconventional guitar techniques.

Include Space and Silence:

Embrace moments of space and silence within your composition. These pauses can add emphasis to certain musical elements and create a sense of tension and release.

Be Open to Evolution:

Allow your composition to evolve naturally during the creative process. Be open to making adjustments, embracing spontaneous ideas, and letting the music guide you.

Record and Reflect:

Record your performances or ideas during the creative process. Listening back allows you to reflect on the strengths of different sections, identify areas for improvement, and refine your composition.

Creating a modal or freeform structure for guitar composition provides an opportunity for artistic freedom and exploration. It's a chance to break away from traditional songwriting norms and delve into a more open and experimental approach.

BLEND STRUCTURES

Combine elements from different structures to create a hybrid form. For example, you can incorporate a verse-chorus structure with a contrasting instrumental section.

CREATING HYBRID STRUCTURES

Blending different chorus-verse structures to create a hybrid form in guitar composition allows for a creative and unique musical expression. This approach involves integrating elements from various songwriting structures, providing flexibility and innovation in crafting engaging compositions.

Hybrid Chorus-Verse Progressions:

Combine elements from different chorus-verse progressions within a single composition. For example, you might use a traditional verse-chorus-verse structure in the first section and transition to an ABAB structure in the second section. This blending can be heard in The Beatles' *A Day in the Life*, where distinct sections contribute to the overall narrative.

Overlapping Sections:

Overlap chorus and verse sections to create seamless transitions. Allow the chorus to subtly emerge during the later part of the verse or introduce a verse melody over the chorus chords.

This technique is employed in Radiohead's *Paranoid Android*, where different sections overlap, creating a continuous flow.

Nested Structures:

Nest one structure within another. For instance, a verse-chorus structure might contain a mini-ABAB structure within the chorus itself. This nested approach can be found in Led Zeppelin's *Stairway to Heaven*, where the long instrumental section is nested within the overall verse-chorus structure.

Varied Instrumentation for Different Sections:

Employ varied instrumentation for different sections to distinguish between them. You can switch between clean and distorted guitar tones, introduce additional instruments, or alter the rhythmic feel. The Smashing Pumpkins' 1979 incorporates a variety of textures and instrumentations within its verse-chorus structure.

Progressive Songwriting:

Embrace a progressive songwriting approach where the composition evolves continuously without strict adherence to traditional structures. Dream Theater's *Octavarium* is an example of a progressive rock piece that seamlessly blends different musical themes, incorporating a variety of structures and styles.

Thematic Continuity:

Establish thematic continuity across different sections. This could involve maintaining a consistent lyrical theme, repeating a signature guitar riff, or using a recurring chord progression. *Bohemian Rhapsody* by Queen exemplifies thematic continuity as it weaves various musical elements into a cohesive whole.

Transitioning Between Styles:

Introduce different stylistic elements within the composition, transitioning between genres or moods. The Red Hot Chili Peppers' *Scar Tissue* combines elements of rock and ballad, seamlessly transitioning between them.

Dynamic Songwriting:

Utilize dynamic songwriting to build tension and release throughout the composition. This may involve shifting between quiet, intimate verses and explosive, anthemic choruses. Pearl Jam's *Alive* incorporates dynamic shifts to enhance its emotional impact.

Experimental Structures:

Embrace experimental structures that defy traditional norms. Tool's *Lateralus* features intricate time signature changes, unconventional structures, and a fluid progression that defies typical songwriting conventions.

Mix of Repetition and Variation:

Combine elements of repetition and variation within your hybrid form. Repeat certain motifs or themes while introducing subtle changes to keep the composition interesting. The Arctic Monkeys' *Do I Wanna Know?* utilizes a repeated guitar riff while evolving dynamically throughout.

Bridging Sections:

Use transitional sections or bridges to connect different structures seamlessly. These bridges can serve as sonic connectors between contrasting elements.

sections or sudden bursts of energy can enhance the impact of the central riff.

Consider Song Length:

Determine the desired length of your composition. Riff-based structures can vary in length, so decide whether you want a concise and punchy piece or a longer exploration of the central theme.

Pay Attention to Timing:

Precise timing is crucial in a riff-based structure. Ensure that the execution of the riff and its variations is tight and well-coordinated, especially if playing with a band.

Experiment with Bridge or Breakdown Sections:

Introduce bridge or breakdown sections where the central riff takes a backseat, allowing for a brief departure from the main theme before returning with renewed intensity.

By following these steps and allowing the central riff to guide the composition, you can create a powerful and memorable guitar piece with a riff-based structure. Whether exploring rock, metal, or other genres, this approach provides a foundation for dynamic and engaging guitar compositions.

MODAL OR FREEFORM STRUCTURES

For a more experimental or improvisational approach, consider modal or freeform structures. These structures provide freedom to explore different tonalities and expressions without strict adherence to traditional forms.

CHARACTERISTICS OF MODAL OR FREEFORM STRUCTURES

Modal or freeform structures in guitar composition deviate from traditional song structures and provide a platform for exploration, improvisation, and creative expression. These structures often prioritize freedom and flexibility, allowing musicians to transcend typical verse-chorus arrangements.

Lack of Traditional Verse-Chorus Form:

Modal or freeform structures typically don't adhere to the conventional verse-chorus-verse format. Instead, they embrace a more open-ended approach.

Emphasis on Improvisation:

These structures often encourage improvisation, allowing musicians to explore different scales, modes, and textures freely.

Extended Instrumental Sections:

Modal compositions may include extended instrumental sections without strict adherence to predetermined song lengths or traditional song sections.

Exploration of Modes and Scales:

Modal structures provide an opportunity to explore various modes and scales, allowing for a broader sonic palette and unique tonalities.

Examples:

Machine Gun (**Jimi Hendrix**):

Jimi Hendrix's *Machine Gun* is an example of a freeform structure. The song, recorded live at the Fillmore East in 1969, features an extended instrumental section where Hendrix explores a variety of guitar textures and improvisational ideas.

Dark Star (**Grateful Dead**):

The Grateful Dead's *Dark Star* is a classic example of a modal structure. The song often served as a platform for extended improvisational performances, with the band exploring different musical landscapes in each rendition.

HOW TO CREATE MODAL OR FREEFORM STRUCTURES FOR GUITAR COMPOSITION

Define the Mood or Theme:

Identify the mood or theme you want to convey in your composition. Without the constraints of a traditional structure, you have the freedom to explore a wide range of emotions and sonic landscapes.

Experiment with Modal Scales:

Choose a modal scale or scales that align with the mood you've defined. Experiment with different modes (e.g., Dorian, Mixolydian, Phrygian) to create unique tonalities and textures.

Establish a Central Motif:

Develop a central motif or musical idea that will serve as the anchor for your composition. This could be a repeating chord progression, a melodic motif, or a rhythmic pattern.

Allow for Improvisation:

Incorporate sections where you or other musicians can improvise freely. This might involve extended solos, call-and-response elements, or collective improvisation.

Explore Dynamic Changes:

Experiment with dynamic changes to create contrast within the composition. This could involve shifts in intensity, volume, or instrumentation to keep the listener engaged.

Consider Non-Linear Progression:

Modal structures often allow for non-linear progression. Consider how the sections of your composition flow into each other, and be open to exploring unexpected transitions.

Utilize Different Textures and Techniques:

Experiment with various guitar textures, techniques, and effects to add sonic variety. This could include variations in volume, intensity, or articulation to add nuance to each section.

Refine Lyrics and Melodies:

Pay close attention to the lyrics and melodies in each section. Ensure that they complement the overall theme of the composition while offering enough contrast to distinguish between A and B.

Experiment with Arrangement:

Experiment with different arrangements and instrumentation to find the most effective presentation for your ABAB structure. Consider how different elements contribute to the overall sound and mood.

By following these steps and drawing inspiration from classic examples, you can create a guitar composition with an ABAB structure that balances repetition and contrast, providing a straightforward yet engaging musical experience.

RIFF-BASED STRUCTURE

If your composition is centered around a distinctive guitar riff, explore a riff-based structure. This approach allows the riff to serve as a recurring motif throughout the piece.

CHARACTERISTICS OF RIFF-BASED STRUCTURE

A riff-based structure in guitar composition revolves around the repetition and development of a central musical motif, often referred to as a "riff." This structure places a strong emphasis on the distinctive and repeated guitar patterns, creating a foundation for the entire composition. Riff-based songs are prevalent in various genres, including rock, metal, blues, and funk.

Prominence of Riffs:

Riffs serve as the focal point of the composition, providing a recognizable and repeated musical idea that defines the entire song.

Repetition and Variation:

Riffs are repeated throughout the composition, maintaining a consistent theme. However, there is often room for variation or development to prevent monotony.

Minimalistic Approach:

Riff-based compositions often adopt a minimalistic approach, focusing on the power and impact of a few key musical ideas rather than complex arrangements.

Instrumental Emphasis:

The guitar, or guitars, take center stage in a riff-based structure. The interplay between various guitar parts is crucial for creating a dynamic and engaging composition.

Examples:

Smoke on the Water (Deep Purple):

The iconic guitar riff in *Smoke on the Water* by Deep Purple is one of the most recognizable in rock history. The song's structure is primarily built around this central riff, creating a straightforward and memorable composition.

Enter Sandman (Metallica):

Enter Sandman by Metallica is another example of a riff-based structure. The main guitar riff is the driving force behind the song, and variations of this riff are used throughout, contributing to the song's intensity.

HOW TO CREATE A RIFF-BASED STRUCTURE FOR GUITAR COMPOSITION

Develop a Strong Riff:

Start by creating a compelling and memorable riff. This can be a series of chords, power chords, or a single-note melody. Ensure that the riff has a distinct and recognizable character.

Explore Variations:

Experiment with variations of the initial riff. This can involve altering the rhythm, adding embellishments, or changing the dynamics. Variations help maintain interest while keeping the central theme intact.

Create Transitions:

Develop smooth transitions between different variations of the riff. Consider using transitional chords, pauses, or drum fills to connect various sections seamlessly.

Build Momentum:

Use the repetition and development of the riff to build momentum throughout the composition. Introduce subtle changes or increases in intensity to create dynamic shifts.

Experiment with Additional Riffs:

Consider incorporating additional riffs to complement the main theme. These secondary riffs can provide contrast and contribute to the overall structure.

Layer Guitar Parts:

If possible, experiment with layering multiple guitar parts. This could involve playing harmonies, counter-melodies, or additional riffs to create a fuller and more textured sound.

Explore Tempo and Dynamics:

Experiment with tempo changes and dynamic variations to add depth to the composition. Slower

COUNTRY

Conventions:

Verse-Chorus Structure: Country songs commonly follow a verse-chorus-verse-chorus-bridge-chorus structure.

Twangy Guitars: The country guitar style often features twangy sounds, pedal steel guitar, and fingerpicking.

Storytelling Themes: Similar to folk, country lyrics often tell stories, and the guitar supports the narrative.

Examples:

Take Me Home, Country Roads (**John Denver**): A country-folk classic with a memorable melody and acoustic guitar accompaniment.

Folsom Prison Blues (**Johnny Cash**): A country-blues song with a simple structure and Cash's distinctive guitar playing.

Understanding the conventions of different guitar composition genres allows musicians to explore diverse songwriting styles. While these conventions provide a framework, many artists creatively blend elements from various genres to craft unique compositions that defy categorization. As you explore these examples and conventions, consider how you can infuse your own creativity and personal style into your guitar compositions.

NARRATIVE ARC

Develop a narrative arc within your composition. Decide how you want the story or emotion to unfold and choose a structure that supports this progression.

STRUCTURING AND NARRATIVE ARC

Developing a narrative arc within your guitar composition involves creating a musical journey that engages the listener and conveys a sense of progression and development. Like a story, your composition can have a beginning, middle, and end, with various elements contributing to a cohesive narrative.

DEFINE THE NARRATIVE THEME

Determine the theme or story you want to convey through your composition. Whether it's an emotion, a personal experience, or an abstract concept, having a clear theme will guide your musical choices.

Establish the Introduction (Exposition):

Melodic Introduction: Begin with a melodic introduction that sets the tone for your composition. This can be a simple guitar riff, chord progression, or a delicate fingerpicked melody.

Define the Mood: Use chords, dynamics, and tonal choices to establish the initial mood. Consider whether you want your composition to start softly and build in intensity or vice versa.

Introduce Musical Elements: Start introducing the main musical elements that will reappear throughout the composition. This could be a recurring motif, a specific chord progression, or a rhythmic pattern.

Build Tension and Develop the Story (Rising Action):

Gradual Intensity: Increase the intensity gradually as your composition progresses. This can involve building up the dynamics, adding layers of instrumentation, or introducing more complex guitar techniques.

Dynamic Changes: Utilize dynamic changes to create peaks and valleys in your narrative. Experiment with loud and soft sections, creating contrasts that contribute to the overall tension.

Modulation or Key Changes: Introduce modulation or key changes to add variety and elevate the emotional impact. Moving to a different key can signal a shift in the narrative.

Reach a Climax (Climax):

Peak Intensity: Build towards a peak intensity point, often referred to as the climax. This could involve a powerful guitar solo, an intricate instrumental section, or a culmination of all the musical elements.

Expressive Playing: Use expressive guitar techniques, such as bending, vibrato, or fast-paced picking, to convey heightened emotions during the climax.

Provide a Moment of Reflection (Falling Action):

Subdued Section: After the climax, bring the intensity down. This section serves as a moment of reflection and allows the listener to absorb the emotional impact of the composition.

Use of Silence or Sustained Notes: Consider incorporating moments of silence or sustained notes to create a sense of space and contemplation.

Build towards Resolution (Resolution):

Reintroduce Earlier Motifs: Bring back earlier motifs or themes from the introduction, creating a sense of resolution and unity within the composition.

Harmonic Resolution: Conclude your composition with a resolution in terms of harmony and tonality. This can involve returning to the original key or resolving to a final chord that provides a sense of closure.

Conclusion (Denouement):

Gentle Fade or Decrescendo: Consider a gradual fade-out or decrescendo to conclude your composition smoothly. This gentle conclusion can leave a lasting impression on the listener.

Reflective Ending: End with a reflective or conclusive phrase, allowing the listener to absorb the narrative arc and experience a sense of completion.

Additional Tips:

Experiment with Tempo Changes: Altering the tempo can create a dynamic shift in your composition, contributing to the narrative arc.

Utilize Different Guitar Techniques: Experiment with a variety of guitar techniques such as fingerpicking, tapping, and slides to add texture and expressiveness.

Incorporate Variations in Articulation: Vary your playing style by experimenting with staccato, legato, and other articulations to convey different emotions.

Example:

Consider David Gilmour's guitar solo in Pink Floyd's *Comfortably Numb*. The solo follows a narrative arc, starting with a melodic and emotive introduction, building tension through expressive playing, reaching a climactic peak, providing a reflective moment, and concluding with a resolution. The solo's narrative quality contributes significantly to the overall impact of the song.

By consciously developing a narrative arc within your guitar composition, you can create a more engaging and emotionally resonant musical experience. Pay attention to the ebb and flow of intensity, utilize various musical elements, and let your creativity guide the storytelling aspect of your guitar playing.

INSTRUMENTATION AND STRUCTURE

Take into account the instrumentation of your composition. If you have specific instrumental sections or solos, choose a structure that allows these elements to shine.

INSTRUMENTATION STRATEGIES

Considering instrumentation is a crucial aspect of crafting a guitar composition, as the chosen structure should allow the instrumentation to shine and serve the overall musical vision.

Identify Key Instruments:

Determine Lead and Supporting Instruments: Identify the primary instruments that will take on lead roles, such as the guitar, and supporting instruments that contribute to the overall texture. Understand their unique characteristics and how they can shine within the composition.

Understand Each Instrument's Strengths:

Explore the Guitar's Range: Understand the guitar's range, tonal capabilities, and various playing techniques. Determine how the guitar can showcase its strengths, whether through melodic lines, chords, or intricate fingerpicking.

Consider Supporting Instruments: If other instruments are involved, such as bass, drums, or additional guitars, explore how they can complement the main guitar's role. Understand their strengths and how they can enhance the overall sound.

Choose a Structure that Allows Instrumental Showcase:

Open Structures for Solos: Consider structures that allow for instrumental showcases, such as solos. A song structure with extended instrumental sections or a dedicated solo portion (e.g., bridge or outro) provides a platform for the guitar to shine.

Instrumental Breaks: Incorporate instrumental breaks within the composition where the guitar can take the spotlight. This could be a section with minimal accompaniment or a moment where the guitar explores melodic and harmonic possibilities.

Experiment with Arrangement and Dynamics:

Dynamic Variations: Utilize dynamic variations to highlight different instruments at various points in the composition. Gradual builds or drops in intensity can emphasize specific instrumental elements.

Experiment with Instrumental Layering: Explore how instruments can interact and layer within the composition. Introduce new elements gradually to create a rich and textured sonic landscape.

Consider the Role of Vocals:

Vocal and Guitar Interplay: If vocals are part of the composition, consider how the guitar can interact with and support the vocal lines. Explore moments where the guitar and vocals complement each other or take turns in the spotlight.

Instrumental Versus Vocal Sections: Designate sections where the vocals take a backseat, allowing the instrumentation, particularly the guitar, to be the focal point. This can create a balanced and engaging listening experience.

Align Structure with Instrumental Complexity:

Match Structure to Technicality: Choose a structure that aligns with the technicality and complexity of the instrumentation. For intricate guitar work, you might opt for a structure that allows for extended instrumental passages and showcases the guitar's technical prowess.

Balance Complexity Across Sections: Ensure a balanced distribution of instrumental complexity across different sections. This could involve a more straightforward verse that contrasts with a complex and dynamic chorus or solo section.

Explore Genres and Styles:

Genre-Specific Considerations: Different genres have unique conventions regarding instrumentation. Explore structures commonly found in your chosen genre and consider how they align with the instruments involved. For example, a blues structure might feature instrumental call-and-response elements, while a progressive rock structure could allow for intricate instrumental interplay.

Test and Refine:

Rehearse and Record: Once you've chosen a structure, rehearse the composition with the intended instrumentation. Record the performance to analyze how each instrument shines within the chosen structure.

Feedback and Adjustments: Seek feedback from bandmates or collaborators and be open to making adjustments. Sometimes small tweaks to the arrangement or structure can enhance the overall impact of the instrumentation.

By carefully considering instrumentation and aligning the structure with the strengths of each instrument, you can create a guitar composition that highlights the unique qualities of the guitar and other supporting instruments. Whether through solos, breaks, or dynamic variations, the chosen structure should serve as a framework for instrumental brilliance and expression.

TRANSITIONS AND STRUCTURE

Pay attention to how you want to transition between sections. Smooth transitions contribute to the cohesiveness of the composition.

Strategies For Transitions

Effectively considering transitions in your song structure is crucial for maintaining flow, coherence, and engagement in your guitar composition. Smooth transitions guide listeners from one section to another, creating a seamless musical experience.

Melodic or Harmonic Connection:

Common Melodic or Harmonic Element: Carry over a melodic or harmonic element from one section to the next. This connection creates cohesion and signals a smooth transition. It could be a recurring motif, chord progression, or melodic phrase.

Chord Progression Pivot: Use a chord that acts as a pivot between sections. This chord should be present in the closing bars of the preceding section and the opening bars of the following section, providing a harmonic bridge.

Gradual Dynamics and Intensity Changes:

Build or Release Tension: Gradually increase or decrease dynamics and intensity as you approach a transition. Building tension before a new section creates anticipation, while releasing tension smoothly leads into a more subdued part.

Dynamic Swells or Fades: Experiment with dynamic swells or fades during transitions. This technique involves gradually increasing or decreasing volume, creating a natural ebb and flow between sections.

Rhythmic Continuity or Variation:

Maintain Rhythmic Continuity: Keep a consistent underlying rhythm or pulse during transitions. This continuity helps maintain a sense of flow even as other elements change.

Syncopation or Rhythmic Shifts: Introduce subtle syncopations or rhythmic shifts during transitions to add interest. This can involve altering the strumming pattern, changing the emphasis on certain beats, or introducing new rhythmic elements.

Effective Use of Silence:

Brief Pauses: Insert brief pauses or moments of silence strategically. This technique creates a sense of anticipation and separation between sections, making the transition more noticeable.

Use of Rests: Incorporate rests within the musical phrases leading up to the transition. A well-placed rest can serve as a punctuation mark, signaling a change in the musical direction.

Transitional Chords or Passing Tones:

Transitional Chords: Introduce transitional chords that help bridge the gap between sections. These chords might serve as a link, containing notes common to both sections.

Passing Tones or Leading Notes: Include passing tones or leading notes that smoothly connect the end of one section to the beginning of the next. These intermediary notes guide the listener through the transition.

Instrumental Fills or Runs:

Guitar Fills or Runs: Employ guitar fills or runs that span the transition between sections. These can serve as expressive embellishments that bridge the gap and add a touch of virtuosity.

Lead Guitar Flourishes: Utilize lead guitar flourishes or embellishments during transitions to maintain interest and showcase the technical abilities of the instrument.

Consideration of Tempo and Time Signature:

Gradual Tempo Changes: Experiment with gradual tempo changes to introduce a new section. This can be particularly effective in genres that allow for flexibility in tempo, such as progressive rock or jazz.

Common Time Signatures: Maintain a common time signature between sections for a smoother transition. If time signature changes are necessary, ensure they are executed seamlessly.

Preparation for Changes:

Anticipatory Build: Build anticipation for a new section by subtly hinting at upcoming changes. This could involve a slight variation in the rhythm or a chord voicing that prepares the listener for the transition.

Use of Crescendos: Gradually increase the volume or intensity leading up to a transition. This crescendo signals a forthcoming change and keeps the listener engaged.

Effective transitions play a pivotal role in enhancing the overall quality of your guitar composition. By strategically implementing melodic connections, dynamic shifts, rhythmic variations, and other techniques, you can create seamless and engaging transitions that contribute to the cohesiveness of your musical narrative. Experiment with these strategies, keeping in mind the overall mood and structure of your composition, to achieve smooth and impactful transitions.

PLAYING STYLE AND STRUCTURE

Consider your own playing style and strengths as a guitarist. Certain structures may naturally complement your unique approach to the instrument.

ASSESSING PLAYING STYLE AND STRENGTH

Reflecting on your playing style and strengths as a guitarist is a valuable process that can significantly inform your approach to song structure in guitar composition.

What Are My Technical Proficiencies?

Question: What specific technical skills do I excel at on the guitar?

Implication for Song Structure: Understanding your technical strengths allows you to incorporate them into various sections of your composition. For example, if you are proficient in fingerpicking, you might feature fingerstyle passages in specific parts of the song.

What Genres or Styles Do I Feel Most Comfortable Playing?

Question: In which genres or styles do I feel most at home as a guitarist?

Implication for Song Structure: Your preferred genres or styles can influence the overall structure of your composition. For instance, blues compositions might lean towards specific progressions and forms, while rock compositions may feature dynamic contrasts and guitar solos.

What Expressive Techniques Do I Enjoy Using?

Question: Which expressive techniques, such as bending, sliding, or vibrato, do I enjoy incorporating into my playing?

Implication for Song Structure: Identifying your favorite expressive techniques allows you to integrate them strategically. Sections with emotional impact, like a bridge or climax, might be ideal for showcasing these techniques to evoke specific feelings.

Am I More Comfortable with Rhythm or Lead Guitar Playing?

Question: Do I gravitate more towards rhythm playing, lead playing, or a balance of both?

Implication for Song Structure: Your comfort zone can influence the distribution of roles within your composition. If you excel at lead playing, you might incorporate more solo sections or instrumental breaks. If rhythm is your strength, you can focus on crafting compelling chord progressions and rhythmic patterns.

What Is My Preferred Guitar Tone and Sound?

Question: What type of guitar tone and sound do I find most appealing?

Implication for Song Structure: Your preferred tone can guide the arrangement and instrumentation choices. If you love clean, jazzy tones, you might design sections that highlight the clarity of your guitar sound. Alternatively, if you prefer distorted tones, you can craft heavier sections for impact.

How Comfortable Am I with Dynamic Playing?

Question: How comfortable am I with varying dynamics in my playing?

Implication for Song Structure: Dynamic contrasts are crucial in songwriting. If you are adept at manipulating dynamics, consider incorporating sections with varying levels of intensity. This could involve moving from quiet verses to explosive choruses or creating subtle shifts within a section.

Do I Enjoy Experimenting with Unconventional Sounds or Tunings?

Question: Am I inclined to experiment with unconventional sounds, alternate tunings, or extended techniques?

Implication for Song Structure: If you enjoy pushing the boundaries of traditional guitar playing, you can use these elements to add uniqueness to your composition. Consider sections where you can showcase experimental sounds or incorporate unconventional techniques.

What Are My Preferred Songwriting Techniques?

Question: Do I have favorite songwriting techniques, such as modulation, key changes, or modal shifts?

Implication for Song Structure: Identifying your preferred songwriting techniques allows you to weave them into the fabric of your composition. Whether it's a subtle key change in a chorus or a modal shift in a solo, incorporating these techniques enhances the complexity and interest of your song structure.

What Role Does Improvisation Play in My Playing?

Question: How comfortable am I with improvisation, and do I enjoy incorporating it into my playing?

Implication for Song Structure: If you enjoy improvisation, consider allocating sections within your composition for expressive, spontaneous playing. This could be a designated solo section or opportunities for improvisational interplay with other instruments.

What Emotional or Conceptual Themes Resonate with My Playing?

Question: Are there specific emotions or conceptual themes that resonate with my playing style?

Implication for Song Structure: Identifying emotional or conceptual themes can guide the lyrical content and overall mood of your composition. It helps in structuring sections that effectively convey the intended emotions or themes.

How Do I Approach Collaborative Playing with Other Musicians?

Question: How do I approach collaboration with other musicians, and how can I incorporate their strengths into the composition?

Analyzing other musicians with a focus on song structures allows you to extract valuable insights and techniques that you can apply to your own guitar compositions. By asking these questions and closely studying various aspects of their compositions, you'll gain a deeper understanding of how to convey emotion and captivate listeners through effective songwriting and arrangement.

REVISION AND STRUCTURE

Be flexible and open to revising your initial structure. As your composition evolves, you may find that certain sections or arrangements work better than others.

OPENNESS TO REVISION

Being open to revising your initial song structure in your guitar composition is a key aspect of the creative process. Embracing flexibility allows you to refine and enhance your work, often leading to a more polished and impactful piece of music.

Embrace the Iterative Nature of Songwriting:

Creative Evolution: Recognize that songwriting is a dynamic, evolving process. Initial ideas may transform and take on new dimensions as you explore different possibilities.

Refinement Over Time: Understand that the first draft of your song structure is a starting point. It's common for compositions to undergo multiple revisions, each contributing to the refinement of your musical vision.

Listen Critically to Your Work:

Objective Evaluation: Listen to your composition objectively. Identify sections that feel less cohesive, moments that could be enhanced, or areas where the emotional impact could be strengthened.

Feedback from Others: Seek feedback from peers, mentors, or collaborators. Fresh perspectives can provide valuable insights and highlight aspects of your composition that might benefit from revision.

Consider Emotional Impact:

Evaluate Emotional Resonance: Assess whether the current structure effectively conveys the intended emotions. If certain sections fall short, be open to restructuring to enhance the emotional impact.

Experiment with Dynamics: Explore variations in dynamics, tempo, and intensity to infuse more emotion into your composition. This may involve rethinking the placement of climactic moments or subtle shifts in mood.

Experiment with Alternative Structures:

Try Different Arrangements: Experiment with alternative arrangements and structures. This can involve swapping sections, changing the order of verses and choruses, or exploring unconventional song structures.

Incorporate Feedback: If you receive feedback suggesting specific changes, be willing to test those suggestions. It doesn't mean you have to adopt every idea, but being open to experimentation can lead to unexpected breakthroughs.

Adapt to the Needs of the Song:

Serve the Song's Essence: Prioritize the essence of the song over sticking rigidly to the initial plan. If a particular section or idea doesn't serve the overall narrative or emotional journey, be willing to adapt or discard it.

Balance Complexity and Simplicity: Assess the balance between complexity and simplicity. Sometimes simplifying a section or adding complexity where needed can enhance the overall composition.

Address Flow and Continuity:

Smooth Transitions: Ensure that transitions between sections are smooth and contribute to the overall flow of the composition. If a transition feels abrupt or disjointed, consider revising the arrangement to create a more seamless connection.

Consistent Themes: Check for consistency in themes and motifs throughout the composition. A cohesive thread running through the song contributes to a unified and engaging listening experience.

Refine Instrumentation and Orchestration:

Optimize Instrumental Choices: Reevaluate your instrumental choices in each section. Consider how the guitar parts interact with other instruments or stand alone. Adjustments to instrumentation can significantly impact the overall sonic landscape.

Enhance Guitar Techniques: Experiment with different guitar techniques, tones, and textures. Refining these elements can elevate your composition, making it more expressive and captivating.

Maintain a Creative Mindset:

Avoid Rigidity: Resist the temptation to become overly attached to your initial ideas. Allow yourself the freedom to explore new possibilities without feeling constrained by your original vision.

Embrace Surprises: Be open to unexpected moments of inspiration. Sometimes, the most memorable aspects of a composition arise during the revision process.

unconventional chord voicings, melodic phrasing, and expressive techniques. The result is a timeless piece that continues to inspire guitarists across genres.

Experimenting and trusting your intuition in guitar composition are pathways to artistic freedom and innovation. By fostering a playful mindset, embracing unconventional techniques, and remaining open to the unexpected, you can infuse your compositions with authenticity and creativity. Remember that the creative journey is unique for each musician, and allowing your intuition to guide you can lead to compositions that reflect your distinct voice as a guitarist.

DETERMINE SECTION LENGTHS

Determining the length of each section in your guitar composition is a crucial aspect of crafting a well-balanced and engaging piece. The length of each section—whether it's a verse, chorus, or bridge—directly influences the overall pacing and structure of your composition.

CONSIDERATION OF LENGTH

Determining the length of each section, including verses, choruses, and bridges, is crucial to the overall song structure of your guitar composition. The length of each section plays a pivotal role in shaping the composition's dynamics, maintaining listener engagement, and conveying the intended emotional journey.

Structural Coherence:

Logical Progression: Determining the length of each section contributes to the overall structural coherence of your composition. It establishes a logical progression from one section to the next, creating a well-organized and easily navigable musical journey.

Clear Definition: Clear distinctions in section lengths help listeners identify and remember different parts of the song. This clarity enhances the overall listening experience, making it more accessible and enjoyable.

Dynamic Contrast:

Variety in Lengths: Varying the length of sections adds dynamic contrast to your composition. For example, shorter verses followed by longer choruses or a brief bridge can create a sense of ebb and flow, keeping the listener engaged through changing dynamics.

Building and Releasing Tension: Manipulating section lengths strategically contributes to building and releasing tension within the composition. This can lead to impactful moments, such as a longer build-up in a bridge before a powerful chorus.

Emotional Impact:

Emotional Resonance: The length of each section can directly impact the emotional resonance of your composition. Longer sections might allow for deeper emotional exploration, while shorter sections can maintain energy and momentum.

Aligning Lengths with Emotion: Consider aligning the length of a section with the intended emotional content. For instance, a shorter, intense chorus may convey a burst of emotion, while a more extended, reflective bridge can allow for a deeper emotional exploration.

Lyrical and Melodic Considerations:

Lyrical Pacing: The length of sections should complement the pacing of your lyrics. Ensure that the lyrical content has enough time to unfold meaningfully, whether through concise verses or expansive choruses.

Melodic Development: Longer sections provide space for melodic development, allowing melodies to evolve and captivate the listener. Consider the interplay between lyrics and melody when determining the length of each section.

Listener Expectations:

Establishing Expectations: Over time, listeners develop expectations regarding section lengths based on the conventions of different genres. While experimentation is encouraged, being mindful of these expectations can help create a comfortable and familiar listening experience.

Subverting Expectations: Deliberately subverting expectations by altering section lengths can add an element of surprise and innovation to your composition. However, it's crucial to balance experimentation with an understanding of your audience's expectations.

Instrumental Showcasing:

Spotlighting Instrumentation: The length of sections can impact how instrumental elements are showcased. Consider allowing extended sections for guitar solos or instrumental breaks, providing an opportunity for the guitar to take the spotlight.

Balancing Instrumental and Vocal Sections: If vocals and guitar play prominent roles, balancing the length of vocal and instrumental sections ensures a harmonious distribution of focus, contributing to a well-rounded composition.

Repetition and Development:

Strategic Repetition: Repetition is a powerful tool in songwriting. Determining section lengths allows you to strategically repeat certain parts for emphasis, reinforcing memorable elements and enhancing the overall structure.

Progressive Development: On the other hand, varying section lengths also enables progressive development. Evolving sections over time keeps the composition dynamic, preventing it from becoming monotonous.

Example:

Consider the song *Hotel California* by Eagles. The verses and choruses have distinct lengths, contributing to the overall narrative structure of the song. The extended instrumental section serves as a bridge, allowing for expressive guitar solos and creating a distinctive musical experience.

The overall song structure plays a role in determining section lengths. For example, in a typical verse-chorus-verse-chorus-bridge-chorus structure, you might aim for a balance between the repetition of familiar sections (verses and choruses) and the unique elements introduced in the bridge.

Determining the length of each section in your guitar composition is a deliberate and thoughtful process that directly influences the overall structure, dynamics, and emotional impact of your music. By carefully considering the pacing, contrast, and alignment with your creative goals, you can create a composition that not only engages the listener but also effectively communicates your musical vision. Experimentation and a willingness to trust your intuition during this process will contribute to the unique and compelling nature of your guitar composition.

CONVENTIONS AND STRUCTURE

Consider common conventions in songwriting. Verses are often shorter than choruses, providing a setup for the more prominent and memorable chorus sections. Bridges, as transitional elements, are typically shorter but serve a crucial role in adding variety.

ALIGN WITH SONGWRITING CONVENTIONS

Defining a song's structure in guitar composition involves considering various conventions that help create a cohesive and engaging musical experience. While creativity allows for flexibility, certain common conventions provide a framework for effective songwriting.

Introductory Section:

Establishing Atmosphere: Begin with an introductory section to set the tone and atmosphere of the song. This section often introduces the main musical themes, creating a sense of anticipation.

Example: The gentle arpeggios in the intro of *Stairway to Heaven* by Led Zeppelin establish a mood before the song unfolds.

Verse-Chorus Structure:

Narrative Flow: The verse-chorus structure is a classic convention. Verses typically convey the narrative, while choruses provide a memorable and repeated hook.

Example: In *Hotel California* by Eagles, the verse-chorus structure is evident, with distinct storytelling in the verses and a memorable chorus.

Pre-Chorus and Bridge Sections:

Transition and Development: Pre-choruses prepare the listener for the chorus, while bridges provide contrast and development, often leading to a climactic point.

Example: The pre-chorus in *With or Without You* by U2 builds tension before the release in the chorus, while the bridge introduces a contrasting element.

Instrumental Breaks and Solos:

Showcasing Musicianship: Incorporate instrumental breaks or solos to showcase guitar skills. These sections can add excitement and variation to the song.

Example: The guitar solo in *Comfortably Numb* by Pink Floyd is a notable example of a well-crafted instrumental break.

Outro or Conclusion:

Gradual Resolution: Provide a conclusion or outro that offers a sense of resolution. This section may revisit earlier themes or introduce new elements for a graceful conclusion.

Example: The outro of *Hey Jude* by The Beatles gradually fades out, creating a sense of closure.

Refrains and Hooks:

Memorable Elements: Incorporate refrains or hooks that are repeated throughout the song. These elements enhance memorability and contribute to the song's identity.

Example: The repeated phrase, *I'm on the highway to hell*, in the chorus of *Highway to Hell* by AC/DC serves as a memorable hook.

Dynamic Contrast:

Variety in Intensity: Create dynamic contrast by varying the intensity between sections. Alternating between softer and louder parts enhances the overall listening experience.

Example: The contrast between the subdued verses and powerful choruses in *Smells Like Teen Spirit* by Nirvana contributes to the song's impact.

Chord Progressions:

Harmonic Variety: Experiment with chord progressions to provide harmonic variety. Common progressions like I–IV–V or ii–V–I can form the backbone of your composition.

Example: The chord progression in *Brown Eyed Girl* by Van Morrison is a classic example of a well-crafted and catchy sequence.

Vocal and Guitar Interplay:

Complementary Roles: Ensure a strong connection between vocal and guitar parts. Consider how the guitar complements the vocal melody and vice versa.

Example: The interplay between the vocal melody and guitar riff in *Blackbird* by The Beatles creates a harmonious relationship.

Trust Your Instincts:

Ultimately, trust your musical instincts. If a particular section length feels right for the mood and emotion you want to convey, go with it. Experimentation is a creative process, and intuition plays a significant role in making artistic decisions.

Remember that experimentation is a dynamic and iterative process. Be open to making adjustments, refining your ideas, and discovering new possibilities as you explore different section lengths in your guitar composition.

VERSE-CHORUS STRUCTURE

Verse-chorus structure gives a familiar and accessible format. This structure is prevalent in pop, rock, and many other genres. Verses build the narrative, and choruses provide a memorable and repeated hook.

EXPLORE VERSE-CHORUS STRUCTURE

Choosing a Verse-Chorus structure for your guitar composition involves considering various elements to ensure cohesiveness and engaging musical storytelling.

Here are some questions to guide your decision-making process:

What is the Core Message or Theme of My Composition?

Consider the central idea or emotion you want to convey. The Verse-Chorus structure is often effective for emphasizing a core message, with verses providing context and choruses delivering the main message.

Do I Have a Strong Chorus Hook?

Assess the strength of your chorus. A powerful and memorable chorus hook can be a driving force in choosing a Verse-Chorus structure, as it becomes a central point for listener engagement and recognition.

Is There a Clear Distinction Between Verses and Choruses?

Ensure that there is a noticeable contrast between your verses and choruses. This contrast can be in terms of dynamics, melody, instrumentation, or lyrics. It contributes to the structure's effectiveness.

Does My Composition Tell a Story?

If your composition follows a narrative or tells a story, the Verse-Chorus structure can provide a clear framework for unfolding the plot. Verses can present details, while choruses deliver key messages or emotional peaks.

Are There Strong Melodic and/or Lyric Differences Between Sections?

Assess whether your verses and choruses offer distinct melodic or lyrical elements. This distinction can enhance the overall structure and make each section memorable.

How Can I Create Buildup and Release Between Verses and Choruses?

Consider how you can build anticipation in the verses and release it in the choruses. Dynamic changes, chord progressions, or lyrical intensity can contribute to an effective buildup and release.

Does the Composition Have Repeatable Elements?

Identify elements that can be repeated, providing a sense of familiarity. Repetition is a key aspect of the Verse-Chorus structure and can aid listener retention.

Do I Want a Catchy and Sing-Along Quality?

If your goal is to create a song with a sing-along quality, the Verse-Chorus structure is often well-suited. The repetition of the chorus allows listeners to easily connect with and participate in the song.

What Emotion or Mood Do I Want to Evoke?

Consider the emotional journey of your composition. How do you want the listener to feel during the verses versus the choruses? Tailor your structure to support the desired emotional impact.

Can I Experiment with Dynamics within the Structure?

Explore how dynamics can be manipulated within the Verse-Chorus framework. This might involve variations in instrumentation, vocal delivery, or intensity to add nuance and interest.

How Long Do I Want My Composition to Be?

Determine the desired length of your composition. The Verse-Chorus structure can be adapted to fit different durations, but understanding your ideal length will help you plan the arrangement.

Is There Room for a Bridge or Instrumental Break?

Decide if your composition could benefit from a bridge or instrumental break between verses and choruses. This can add variety and serve as a transitional element.

Does the Structure Serve the Genre I'm Working In?

Consider whether the Verse-Chorus structure aligns with the conventions of the genre you're working in. Some genres may favor or require certain structural elements.

Have I Listened Critically to Similar Songs in the Genre?

Analyze songs in your chosen genre that follow a Verse-Chorus structure. Pay attention to how they handle transitions, dynamics, and the overall balance between verses and choruses.

Asking these questions and critically evaluating your composition based on these considerations will guide you in making informed decisions about whether a Verse-Chorus structure is the most suitable framework for your guitar composition.

AABA STRUCTURE

Opt for an AABA structure if you want a more complex and traditional form. This structure often involves presenting a main theme (A), introducing a contrasting section (B), and returning to the main theme (A) with a slight variation.

EXPLORING ABBA STRUCTURE

The AABA structure is a popular songwriting format that consists of four sections: two identical A sections, a contrasting B section, and a return to the initial A section. This structure provides a sense of familiarity and repetition while introducing variation and interest. It's widely used in various genres, including jazz, pop, and blues.

A Section:

The first A section introduces the main melody, chords, and lyrics. This section establishes the primary theme of the composition.

A Section (Repeat):

The second A section repeats the material from the first A section with little to no variation. This repetition creates a sense of familiarity for the listener.

B Section:

The B section provides contrast to the A sections. It introduces new melodies, chords, or lyrics that deviate from the established theme. The B section is often referred to as the "bridge."

A Section (Return):

The final A section revisits the original theme, bringing the composition full circle. This return to the familiar reinforces the main idea and provides a satisfying sense of resolution.

Examples:

Somewhere Over the Rainbow (**Harold Arlen and E.Y. Harburg**):
A Section: *Somewhere over the rainbow, way up high*
B Section: *Someday I'll wish upon a star*
A Section (Return): *Somewhere over the rainbow, bluebirds fly*
In this classic song, the AABA structure is evident, with the A sections expressing the desire for a better place and the B section introducing the idea of wishing upon a star.

Fly Me to the Moon (**Bart Howard**):
A Section: *Fly me to the moon, and let me play among the stars*
B Section: *In other words, hold my hand*
A Section (Return): *Fill my heart with song and let me sing forevermore*
Fly Me to the Moon features the AABA structure, where the A sections express the desire for a romantic journey to the moon, while the B section introduces the concept of holding hands.

HOW TO CREATE AN AABA STRUCTURE

Develop a Strong A Section:

Create a memorable melody, chord progression, and lyrics for the initial A section. This will serve as the foundation for your composition.

Repeat the A Section:

Repeat the A section to reinforce the main theme. You can keep it identical or make subtle variations to maintain interest.

Introduce a Contrasting B Section:

Develop a contrasting B section that introduces new musical and lyrical elements. Experiment with different chords, melodies, and rhythms to create contrast.

Ensure a Smooth Transition:

Ensure a smooth transition between the B section and the final A section. Consider using transitional chords or a brief instrumental passage to connect the sections seamlessly.

Finalize the Return to A:

Bring the composition full circle by returning to the original A section. This return should feel satisfying and provide a sense of resolution.

Experiment with Arrangement and Instrumentation:

Experiment with different arrangements and guitar techniques to enhance each section. Consider dynamics, strumming patterns, fingerpicking, or solos to add variety within the AABA structure.

By following these steps and drawing inspiration from classic examples, you can create a compelling guitar composition with an AABA structure that combines familiarity and contrast for an engaging musical experience.

ABAB STRUCTURE

Consider an ABAB structure for simplicity and balance. This structure alternates between two distinct sections, offering a straightforward and easily digestible format.

ABAB STRUCTURE OVERVIEW

The ABAB structure is a common and straightforward songwriting format that consists of two distinct sections (A and B) that alternate throughout the composition. Each section typically has its own unique melody, chords, and lyrics, providing contrast and variation. This structure is prevalent in various genres and allows for simplicity and repetition while maintaining listener interest.

A Section:

The first A section introduces the main musical and lyrical theme of the composition.

B Section:

The B section contrasts with the A section, presenting new melodies, chords, or lyrics. This section provides a departure from the initial theme.

A Section (Repeat):

The second A section returns to the original theme, creating a sense of familiarity and completing the cycle.

Examples:

Wish You Were Here (Pink Floyd):

A Section: Acoustic guitar riff with lyrics reflecting on absence and longing.
B Section: Slide guitar solo with a different chord progression and melody.
A Section (Repeat): Reintroduction of the original acoustic guitar riff and lyrics.
In *Wish You Were Here*, the ABAB structure is evident as the song alternates between the acoustic guitar-driven A sections and the slide guitar-driven B section.

Wonderwall (Oasis):

A Section: Iconic guitar strumming pattern with lyrics expressing a mix of melancholy and hope.
B Section: Slight shift in chord progression and lyrics offering a contrast to the initial theme.
A Section (Repeat): Return to the original strumming pattern and lyrics.
Wonderwall follows the ABAB structure, featuring distinct A and B sections that contribute to the song's dynamic appeal.

HOW TO CREATE AN ABAB STRUCTURE FOR GUITAR COMPOSITION

Establish a Strong A Section:

Develop a compelling melody, chord progression, and lyrics for the first A section. This section sets the foundation for your composition.

Introduce a Contrasting B Section:

Create a B section that contrasts with the A section. Experiment with different chords, melodies, and lyrics to provide variety and capture the listener's attention.

Ensure Smooth Transitions:

Craft smooth transitions between the A and B sections. Consider using transitional chords or a brief instrumental passage to connect the sections seamlessly.

Repeat the A Section:

Bring the composition full circle by returning to the original A section. This repetition establishes familiarity and reinforces the main theme.

Experiment with Guitar Techniques:

Explore various guitar techniques within each section to add depth and interest. Experiment with strumming patterns, fingerpicking, arpeggios, or solos to enhance the overall composition.

Consider Dynamic Changes:

Introduce dynamic changes within the A and B sections to keep the listener engaged. Experiment with

Continuous Evaluation:

Regularly listen to and evaluate your composition in terms of dynamics. Ensure that the dynamic choices align with the intended mood and emotion. Make adjustments as needed to refine the expressive qualities.

Performance Dynamics:

If you're performing your composition live, practice controlling dynamics during your performance. Experiment with playing softer or louder to gauge the audience's response and adjust accordingly.

By consciously considering the mood and dynamics in your guitar composition, you can elevate the emotional impact of your music. Experiment with different dynamic choices, and allow your creativity to guide you in shaping a captivating and expressive piece.

SECTION LENGTHS

Experiment with different lengths for your sections (verses, choruses, bridges). Adjusting the duration of each section can impact the overall pacing and feel of your composition.

EXPERIMENTING WITH SECTION LENGTHS

Experimenting with section lengths in your guitar composition is an effective way to add variety, maintain listener engagement, and create a dynamic structure.

There are several strategies you can employ to determine section lengths for your guitar composition. Let's dive in!

Understand Traditional Section Lengths:
Familiarize yourself with common section lengths in music, such as typical verse and chorus lengths. This understanding provides a foundation for experimentation.

Start with a Basic Structure:
Begin your composition with a basic structure, such as a traditional verse-chorus-verse pattern. This gives you a framework to deviate from and experiment with.

Vary the Length of Verses and Choruses:
Try altering the length of your verses and choruses. For example, extend a verse to create a more immersive storytelling experience or shorten a chorus to add a sense of urgency.

Explore Uneven Section Lengths:

Break away from symmetrical structures by experimenting with uneven section lengths. Instead of having equal-length verses and choruses, consider having a shorter verse followed by a longer chorus, or vice versa.

Insert Interludes or Bridges:

Introduce interludes or bridge sections with varying lengths. These segments can provide a break from the main themes and contribute to the overall flow of the composition.

Use Repetition Strategically:

Experiment with repetition to create longer sections. Repeating certain phrases or musical ideas can extend the length of a section while maintaining a sense of familiarity.

Consider Instrumental Breaks:

Incorporate instrumental breaks of varying lengths to showcase your guitar skills and add diversity to the composition. These breaks can serve as transitional elements between sections.

Experiment with Pre-Choruses:

Insert pre-choruses of different lengths to build anticipation before the main chorus. A shorter pre-chorus may create a quick buildup, while a longer one can heighten tension.

Play with Dynamics within Sections:

Experiment with dynamic changes within sections to create contrast and maintain interest. A section might start quietly and gradually build in intensity, or vice versa.

Explore Non-Linear Structures:

Break away from linear structures by experimenting with non-traditional forms. Consider a structure where sections are rearranged, repeated in a different order, or even looped in a unique way.

Think About Overall Composition Length:

Consider the total length of your composition. If you have a shorter piece, shorter sections might contribute to a concise and impactful experience, while longer compositions may benefit from more varied and extended sections.

Listen and Evaluate:

Regularly listen to your composition and evaluate how different section lengths impact the overall flow and emotional arc. Pay attention to the pacing and ensure that each section serves its purpose within the larger context of the composition.

Seek Feedback:

Share your composition with others and gather feedback. External perspectives can offer valuable insights into the effectiveness of your chosen section lengths and structures.

Use of Dynamics and Tempo Changes:

Expressive Elements: Experiment with dynamics and tempo changes to add expressive elements. Building tension and releasing it through changes in intensity can be particularly effective.

Example: The use of dynamics in *Wish You Were Here* by Pink Floyd contributes to the emotional impact of the song.

While these conventions provide a solid foundation, it's important to approach song structure with a balance of tradition and innovation. Feel free to experiment with these elements, combine them in unique ways, and allow your creativity to guide the process. By understanding these conventions, you can effectively define a song's structure in your guitar compositions while leaving room for artistic expression and individuality.

CHORUS IMPACT AND LENGTH

The chorus is often the emotional and melodic peak of a song. Make sure the chorus has enough time to develop and leave a lasting impression. A chorus that is too short may not have the desired impact.

EMPHASIZE CHORUS IMPACT

Emphasizing the impact of the chorus is a crucial aspect of song structure in guitar composition. The chorus is often considered the emotional and melodic centerpiece of a song, and its impact can significantly influence the overall listening experience.

Here are some strategies to consider to emphasize the chorus impact in your guitar compositions.

Melodic Distinction:

Memorable Melodies: Craft a chorus with a distinctive and memorable melody. The goal is to create a section that stands out and remains in the listener's mind.

Vocal-Guitar Synergy: Ensure that the melody in the chorus complements the vocal line. The synergy between vocals and guitar enhances the overall impact.

Dynamic Intensity:

Buildup to Chorus: Create a sense of anticipation leading up to the chorus. Gradually increase the intensity by incorporating dynamics, such as a rise in volume, strumming intensity, or adding layers to the arrangement.

Contrast with Verses: Make sure there's a noticeable contrast in dynamics between the verses and the chorus.

This contrast emphasizes the emotional release when the chorus hits.

Lyrically Resonant Choruses:

Emotional Core: Craft choruses with lyrics that encapsulate the emotional core of the song. The chorus often serves as the emotional climax, and resonant lyrics enhance its impact.

Repetition for Emphasis: Use repetition strategically in the chorus lyrics. Repeating key phrases or themes reinforces the emotional message and makes the section more impactful.

Instrumental Buildup:

Guitar Prowess: If applicable, showcase guitar prowess during the buildup to the chorus. Consider incorporating a guitar solo, powerful riffs, or expressive techniques that elevate the musical intensity.

Gradual Crescendo: Build up the instrumental arrangement gradually, introducing layers and textures that culminate in the full expression of the chorus.

Harmonic Intensity:

Harmonic Changes: Introduce harmonic changes as the song progresses toward the chorus. This could involve a key change, modulation, or the introduction of new chords to heighten the harmonic intensity.

Chord Progression Impact: Craft a chord progression for the chorus that has a sense of resolution and emotional impact. The right chord choices can amplify the overall effectiveness of the section.

Strategic Instrumentation:

Instrumental Arrangement: Pay attention to the instrumentation during the chorus. Ensure that the arrangement supports the heightened emotion, whether through power chords, arpeggios, or a combination of guitar techniques.

Distinctive Guitar Hooks: Introduce distinctive guitar hooks or motifs in the chorus. These hooks contribute to the memorability of the section and create a sonic signature.

Striking Rhythmic Patterns:

Dynamic Rhythms: Experiment with dynamic rhythmic patterns in the chorus. This can involve variations in strumming patterns, palm muting, or percussive elements that add excitement to the section.

Syncopation and Accentuation: Use syncopation and accentuation to create rhythmic interest. These elements can make the chorus rhythmically engaging and impactful.

Strategic Arrangement Choices:

Build and Release: Arrange the song structure to build tension leading into the chorus and release that tension when the chorus hits. Consider the placement of instrumental breaks or pauses for maximum impact.

Dynamic Arrangement Shifts: Experiment with dynamic shifts in the arrangement, such as sudden drops in instrumentation right before the chorus or a sudden surge in energy.

Vocal Harmony Arrangements:

Harmonizing Vocals: If your composition includes vocal harmonies, use them strategically in the chorus. Vocal harmonies add depth and richness, enhancing the emotional impact of the section.

Layered Vocals: Experiment with layering vocals to create a fuller sound. This can involve doubling the lead vocals, adding backing vocals, or employing other vocal production techniques.

Example:

Consider the song *Livin' on a Prayer* by Bon Jovi. The chorus features a memorable melody, powerful vocal delivery, and a distinctive guitar riff. The arrangement builds up to the chorus, creating a dynamic shift that highlights the emotional core of the song.

Emphasizing the impact of the chorus is a key strategy in creating a memorable and emotionally resonant guitar composition. By carefully crafting the melody, dynamics, lyrics, and arrangement surrounding the chorus, you can ensure that it becomes the focal point of your song, leaving a lasting impression on your audience. Experiment with these techniques to find the right balance that suits the emotional and stylistic goals of your composition.

DYNAMICS AND SECTION LENGTH

Experiment with varying section lengths to create dynamics in your composition. A longer verse followed by a shorter chorus or vice versa can add interest and maintain listener engagement.

CONTRIBUTION OF DYNAMICS TO SECTION LENGTH

Section lengths play a crucial role in shaping the dynamics of a song structure in guitar composition. The duration of each section, including verses, choruses, bridges, and instrumental breaks, directly influences the overall dynamic flow of the composition.

Establishing a Dynamic Framework:

Varied Section Lengths: By incorporating varied section lengths, you establish a dynamic framework within the song. Shorter sections might create a sense of urgency or excitement, while longer sections allow for exploration and development.

Dramatic Contrasts: Sharp contrasts in section lengths contribute to dynamic shifts, preventing monotony and maintaining listener interest. For example, a short, intense verse followed by a longer, more expansive chorus creates a dynamic ebb and flow.

Building and Releasing Tension:

Gradual Buildup: Longer sections, especially in bridges or pre-choruses, can serve as a gradual buildup of tension. This buildup sets the stage for a climactic release, often found in a powerful chorus or guitar solo.

Shorter Release Sections: Conversely, shorter sections can act as immediate releases of tension, injecting energy into the composition. Quick transitions from longer to shorter sections enhance the overall dynamic impact.

Enhancing Emotional Resonance:

Extended Emotional Exploration: Longer sections, such as extended instrumental breaks or reflective bridges, provide more time for emotional exploration. This allows the listener to immerse themselves in the mood and sentiment conveyed by the music.

Quick Emotional Hits: Shorter sections, like punchy verses or impactful choruses, deliver quick emotional hits. The brevity of these sections can create immediate emotional connections, especially in more upbeat or energetic compositions.

Creating Momentum:

Propelling the Song Forward: Varying section lengths contributes to the sense of momentum within a composition. Longer sections propel the song forward, while strategically placed shorter sections act as points of acceleration or emphasis.

Strategic Placement: Experiment with the placement of longer and shorter sections to control the pacing of the song. For example, a shorter, high-energy section might be strategically placed before a longer, more contemplative one.

Balancing Complexity and Simplicity:

Complexity in Extended Sections: Longer sections allow for more intricate musical developments, such as complex guitar solos, intricate chord progressions, or extended instrumental arrangements.

Simplicity in Brief Sections: Shorter sections can embrace simplicity, allowing for a direct and straightforward delivery of the song's core themes. This simplicity can be particularly effective in conveying immediate and impactful messages.

Creating Contrast in Instrumentation:

Instrumental Variation: Section lengths impact how instrumentation is showcased. Longer sections may allow for extended guitar solos or instrumental explorations, while shorter sections can highlight specific guitar riffs or rhythmic patterns.

Balanced Instrumental Presence: Balancing longer and shorter sections ensures that the guitar is showcased effectively throughout the composition. This creates a harmonious blend of instrumental elements that contributes to overall dynamics.

Enhancing Song Structure:

Dynamic Song Arc: Well-planned section lengths contribute to the overall arc of the song. Consider how the dynamics evolve from the beginning to the end, incorporating peaks and valleys that maintain listener engagement.

Transitions as Dynamic Elements: Transitions between sections, especially if they vary in length, serve as dynamic elements that guide the listener through different emotional and sonic landscapes.

Example:

Consider the song *November Rain* by Guns N' Roses. The extended length of the song allows for a gradual build-up, with longer instrumental sections contributing to the overall dynamic range. The contrast between the extended instrumental portions and more concise vocal-driven sections creates a dynamic and engaging listening experience.

Section lengths are a powerful tool in shaping the dynamics of a guitar composition. By strategically manipulating the duration of verses, choruses, bridges, and instrumental breaks, you can create a dynamic and emotionally resonant musical journey. Experimentation with section lengths allows for a nuanced expression of your creative ideas, providing a compelling and engaging experience for the listener.

LYRIC AND MELODIC CONTENT AND SECTION LENGTH

The lyrical and melodic content of each section can influence its length. If a section contains intricate lyrics or a captivating melody, it may warrant a longer duration to allow the listener to fully absorb the content.

INFLUENCE OF LYRICAL AND MELODIC CONTENT

The interplay between lyrical and melodic content has a significant impact on determining the length of each section in a guitar composition's song structure. The content, emotion, and delivery of lyrics and melodies contribute to the overall feel and dynamic flow of the composition.

Verse-Length Determined by Lyric Density:

Lyrically Rich Verses: If your verses are lyrically dense, filled with storytelling or detailed narratives, consider a longer duration. This allows the listener to absorb the content and connect with the story.

Balancing Complexity: If the lyrics are complex, the melody may need more time to unfold. This complexity could involve intricate storytelling, vivid imagery, or detailed character development.

Example: Bob Dylan's *Desolation Row* features lengthy verses with intricate lyrics, allowing the narrative to unfold gradually.

Conciseness in Choruses for Memorability:

Catchy Choruses: Choruses often serve as the song's focal point, and concise, memorable lyrics are crucial. Keeping choruses relatively short ensures their catchiness and makes them easy for listeners to sing along with.

Melodic Hooks: Strong melodic hooks in the chorus can enhance memorability, allowing for repeated exposure without becoming monotonous.

Example: The chorus of *Wonderwall* by Oasis is concise yet memorable, with a straightforward and singable melody.

Extended Bridges for Emotional Depth:

Exploration of Themes: If the bridge contains themes that require deeper exploration or emotional expression, consider an extended length. This allows for a more nuanced delivery of both lyrical and melodic content.

Instrumental Interplay: Bridges often provide opportunities for expressive guitar work, complementing the emotional depth of the lyrics. The melodic content in a longer bridge can support this instrumental interplay.

Example: In Pink Floyd's *Comfortably Numb*, the bridge features an extended guitar solo, adding emotional depth to the composition.

Pre-Chorus Length for Buildup:

Building Anticipation: Pre-choruses often serve as a buildup to the chorus, creating anticipation. The length of the pre-chorus can influence the degree of tension and excitement leading into the main melodic and lyrical statement.

Example: The pre-chorus in U2's *With or Without You* builds anticipation with a gradual increase in intensity before the release in the chorus.

Instrumental Breaks for Musical Expression:

Expressive Instrumentation: Instrumental breaks provide a canvas for musical expression. The length of an instrumental break may be influenced by the complexity and emotional depth of the melodies played on the guitar.

Allowing Guitar Solos: If the section includes a guitar solo, the length is often determined by the guitarist's improvisational skills and the desire to convey a particular emotional message.

Example: In *Hotel California* by Eagles, the instrumental break features a guitar solo that contributes to the song's narrative.

Outro Length for Gradual Conclusion:

Concluding Themes: The outro serves as the conclusion of the song. If the outro contains themes that need a gradual resolution or reflection, a longer length may be appropriate.

Example: The outro of The Beatles' *Hey Jude* is extended, allowing for the gradual fading of the repeated refrain.

Dynamic Shifts for Section Length Variation:

Dynamic Changes in Sections: The dynamics of the song can be accentuated by varying section lengths. A sudden shift from a shorter, energetic section to a longer, contemplative one can create a powerful impact.

Example: Led Zeppelin's *Stairway to Heaven* features dynamic shifts in section lengths, contributing to the epic nature of the composition.

The lyrical and melodic content of each section plays a pivotal role in determining its length within the song structure of a guitar composition. Balancing the depth of storytelling, emotional expression, and musical intricacy with the appropriate section length ensures a cohesive and engaging listening experience.

Consider the narrative arc, emotional intensity, and thematic development when crafting the length of each section, allowing the lyrical and melodic content to guide the dynamic flow of your guitar composition.

ENERGY LEVELS AND SECTION LENGTH

Consider the energy levels of each section. Choruses often have higher energy levels, while verses may be more subdued. The length of each section should align with the desired energy flow throughout the composition.

DETERMINING DESIRED ENERGY FLOW

Determining the length of each section in a guitar composition is a crucial aspect of shaping the overall energy flow. It involves a thoughtful consideration of the desired emotional arc, dynamic contrasts, and the overall listening experience.

Consider these questions when deciding how the length of each section should align with the desired energy flow throughout the composition.

What Emotion or Mood Am I Trying to Convey?

Question: What is the primary emotion or mood I want to convey in each section?

Consideration: The emotional content of each section can guide its length. More emotionally charged sections might benefit from longer durations for depth and exploration.

Where Do I Want Peaks and Valleys in Energy?

Question: Where should the high-energy peaks and more subdued valleys be in my composition?

Consideration: Varying section lengths helps create dynamic peaks and valleys in the energy flow. Shorter, energetic sections can build anticipation for longer, more emotive ones.

What is the Main Focal Point of the Song?

Question: What part of the song do I want to be the focal point—verses, choruses, bridges, or instrumental breaks?

Consideration: Adjust the length of sections based on their importance in conveying the main message or musical theme. For example, choruses are often shorter for memorability.

How Can I Build Tension and Release Effectively?

Question: How can I strategically build tension and release it throughout the song?

Consideration: Longer sections, such as bridges, can be effective for building tension, while shorter sections, like choruses, provide releases. Experiment with different section lengths to achieve the desired tension and release dynamics.

Is There a Specific Story or Narrative I'm Telling?

Question: Does my composition follow a specific narrative or story?

Consideration: If your song tells a story, align section lengths with key moments in the narrative. Longer sections might correspond to pivotal points, while shorter ones can serve as transitions.

Where Do I Want Instrumental Showcases?

Question: Do I want specific sections to showcase instrumental prowess, such as guitar solos or intricate arrangements?

Consideration: Instrumental showcases often benefit from longer sections, allowing for expressive playing. Shorter sections can lead into or follow instrumental highlights.

How Can I Maintain Listener Engagement?

Question: How can I keep the listener engaged from start to finish?

Consideration: Avoid monotony by incorporating a variety of section lengths. Shorter, impactful sections maintain interest, while longer ones provide depth and exploration.

Are There Genre Conventions I Want to Embrace or Subvert?

Question: Does my composition align with or subvert genre conventions regarding section lengths?

Consideration: Different genres may have established norms for section lengths. Consider whether you want to adhere to these conventions or challenge expectations for a unique listening experience.

What Role Does Each Section Play in the Overall Structure?

Question: How does each section contribute to the overall structure and message of the song?

Consideration: Sections with a more pivotal role in the song's structure or message may warrant longer durations. Evaluate the significance of each section in the context of the composition.

How Can I Surprise and Captivate the Listener?

Question: Where can I introduce surprises or unexpected elements to captivate the listener?

Consideration: Unexpected shifts in section lengths can surprise and captivate the listener. Consider strategically altering section lengths for moments of intrigue.

Do I Want to Experiment with Section Lengths to Create Uniqueness?

Question: Am I open to experimenting with unconventional section lengths to create a unique composition?

Consideration: Embrace experimentation to create a distinctive sound. Break away from conventional structures and explore how non-traditional section lengths impact the overall energy flow.

Example:

If you're aiming for a powerful climax in the chorus, you might ask yourself:

How can I build anticipation leading into the chorus?

Would a shorter, punchy verse be more effective in contrast to a longer, soaring chorus?

Do I want to extend the instrumental break before the chorus to intensify the buildup?

Asking these questions and considering their implications can guide you in determining the length of each section in your guitar composition. The interplay between section lengths is a dynamic aspect of songwriting that allows you to craft a composition with a nuanced and engaging energy flow. Trust your instincts, experiment, and use these questions as a foundation to create a compelling and emotionally resonant musical journey.

SONG NARRATIVE AND SECTION LENGTH

If your composition tells a story or has a narrative arc, let the narrative dictate the lengths of the sections. Ensure that each section serves its purpose in advancing the story or conveying the intended emotions.

SERVING THE SONG'S NARRATIVE

The narrative of a song, encompassing its lyrics and overall story arc, has a profound influence on dictating the lengths of different sections in the song structure of a guitar composition. Crafting a cohesive narrative through intentional section lengths enhances the storytelling aspect of the song.

Let's explore how the narrative can guide the lengths of various sections.

Verses:

Storytelling Depth: Longer verses may be appropriate when the narrative demands in-depth storytelling. This allows for the development of characters, events, or themes.

Descriptive Imagery: If the lyrics include vivid imagery or detailed descriptions, longer verses provide the necessary canvas for painting a rich narrative.

Example: Bob Dylan's *Tangled Up in Blue* features lengthy verses that contribute to the narrative complexity and detailed storytelling.

Choruses:

Emotional Peaks: Shorter choruses may work well for delivering emotional peaks. Concise, impactful lines can capture the essence of the narrative and serve as memorable refrains.

Repetition for Emphasis: If certain themes or emotions are central to the narrative, a shorter chorus with repeated lines can emphasize key elements.

Example: In Adele's *Someone Like You*, the chorus is relatively short but emotionally resonant, emphasizing the heartbreak central to the song's narrative.

Bridges:

Turning Points: Longer bridges may be effective for serving as turning points in the narrative. Use this section to introduce new perspectives, plot twists, or emotional shifts.

Character Development: If the narrative involves character development or a change in perspective, a longer bridge provides space for exploring these elements.

Example: The bridge in Taylor Swift's *Love Story* serves as a narrative twist, bringing a change in perspective within the song's storytelling.

Pre-Choruses:

Building Anticipation: Consider shorter pre-choruses for building anticipation before a chorus. Use them to set the stage for the emotional impact that the chorus will deliver.

Foreshadowing: If there's foreshadowing or a hint of what's to come in the chorus, a shorter pre-chorus can create a sense of intrigue.

Example: The pre-chorus in U2's *With or Without You* builds anticipation and foreshadows the emotional release in the chorus.

Instrumental Breaks:

Narrative Pause: Short or extended instrumental breaks can serve as pauses in the narrative, allowing listeners to reflect on the story or providing a musical interlude between lyrical sections.

Emotional Resonance: If there's a need for emotional resonance without lyrics, a longer instrumental break can convey the narrative's mood.

Example: The instrumental break in Pink Floyd's *Comfortably Numb* contributes to the song's overall narrative, providing a moment of introspection.

Outros:

Resolution or Reflection: Longer outros may be suitable for offering resolution or reflection on the narrative. They can provide closure to the story, allowing listeners to absorb the song's themes.

Musical Reflection: If the narrative has concluded, a longer outro can offer a space for instrumental reflection, tying together the emotional journey.

Example: The extended outro of The Beatles' *Hey Jude* serves as a reflective conclusion, repeating the song's uplifting message.

Dynamic Section Length Changes:

Narrative Peaks and Valleys: Align section lengths with the narrative's peaks and valleys. Longer sections during climactic moments and shorter ones during moments of reflection or transition.

Pacing the Story: Use changes in section lengths to control the pacing of the narrative. Longer sections may provide a slow, deliberate pace, while shorter ones can quicken the storytelling.

Example: Led Zeppelin's *Stairway to Heaven* features dynamic shifts in section lengths, aligning with the unfolding narrative and musical intensity.

In guitar composition, allowing the narrative to dictate the lengths of sections adds depth and meaning to the song. By aligning section lengths with the story's demands, you create a musical journey that enhances the listener's engagement with the narrative. As you craft your guitar composition, consider how each section contributes to the overarching narrative and adjust the lengths accordingly to achieve a cohesive and emotionally resonant result.

DYNAMIC CONTRAST AND SECTION LENGTH

Leverage dynamic contrast between sections to maintain listener interest. For example, if a verse is mellow and contemplative, a shorter, more intense chorus can create a compelling contrast.

USING DYNAMIC CONTRAST BETWEEN SECTIONS

Using dynamic contrast between sections is a powerful technique in guitar composition to maintain listener interest and create a compelling musical journey. Dynamic shifts engage the audience, keeping them attentive and emotionally invested.

Varying Intensity and Volume:

Buildup and Release: Gradually increase the intensity and volume leading into a chorus or climactic section. This builds anticipation. Conversely, reduce intensity and volume for softer sections or verses, creating a sense of release.

Strategic Dynamics: Experiment with a mix of loud and soft dynamics. This can involve using crescendos, decrescendos, or sudden shifts in volume to make the transitions between sections more dynamic and engaging.

Differences in Instrumentation:

Full vs. Stripped Down Arrangements: Alternate between full-band arrangements and stripped-down versions to create contrast. A full sound in choruses can contrast effectively with more minimalist verses, maintaining listener interest.

Instrumental Variation: Change the instrumentation between sections. For example, introduce a prominent guitar riff or solo in a chorus, contrasting with simpler chord progressions in verses.

Tempo and Rhythmic Changes:

Tempo Shifts: Experiment with tempo changes between sections. A faster tempo can inject energy, while a slower tempo can add emotional depth. Use tempo shifts strategically to highlight different parts of the song.

Rhythmic Complexity: Vary rhythmic patterns to create contrast. Consider intricate rhythms or syncopated patterns in energetic sections and simpler, straightforward rhythms in more relaxed parts.

Tonal and Harmonic Variations:

Key Changes: Explore key changes between sections to add variety and interest. A key change can signal a new chapter in the song, providing a fresh perspective.

Harmonic Complexity: Introduce harmonic complexity in certain sections. Experiment with unusual chord progressions or modal shifts to create sonic interest and captivate the listener's ear.

Lyrically and Melodically Distinctive Sections:

Lyrically Impactful Choruses: Craft choruses with impactful and memorable lyrics. Use a distinct melodic line that stands out from the verses. The contrast makes the chorus more memorable and emotionally resonant.

Vocal Delivery Variations: Change vocal delivery styles between sections. Consider softer, more intimate vocals in verses and powerful, soaring vocals in choruses.

Duration and Section Lengths:

Varying Section Lengths: Experiment with the lengths of different sections. Short, punchy verses can lead into longer, more expansive choruses, creating a dynamic contrast in duration.

Dynamic Transitions: Use short transitional sections with unique characteristics to smooth the shift between contrasting parts, serving as bridges that prepare the listener for the change.

Contrasting Song Dynamics:

Verse-Chorus Dynamics: Make the contrast between verses and choruses pronounced. Choruses often signify a peak in energy and intensity, creating a dynamic shift from the verses.

Bridge Dynamics: Bridges offer an opportunity for a contrasting dynamic shift. This section can serve as a breath of fresh air or a moment of tension before a powerful resolution.

Instrumental Breaks and Solos:

Dynamic Instrumental Breaks: Utilize instrumental breaks or solos strategically to create dynamic contrast. These sections can showcase the guitar's versatility and add excitement.

Contrasting Moods: If an instrumental break follows an intense chorus, consider shifting the mood to something more introspective or subdued before returning to a high-energy section.

Example:

Consider Metallica's *Master of Puppets*. The song features dynamic contrast through its shifting tempos, intense guitar riffs, and softer interludes. The juxtaposition of heavy sections and quieter moments adds depth to the overall composition.

Dynamic contrast is a key element in creating an engaging and memorable guitar composition. By strategically manipulating intensity, volume, instrumentation, tempo, and other musical elements, you can captivate your audience's attention and guide them through a dynamic and emotionally resonant musical journey. Experiment with these techniques to discover the unique sonic palette that best suits your artistic vision.

REPETITION AND SECTION LENGTH

Experiment with repetition within sections. Repeating certain phrases or chord progressions can create familiarity, but be mindful not to overuse repetition, as it may lead to predictability.

EXPERIMENTING WITH REPETITION

Experimenting with repetition within sections is a dynamic aspect of song structure in guitar composition. Repetition can serve various purposes, from creating familiarity to emphasizing key elements within a section.

Emphasizing Hooks and Riffs:

Repeating Catchy Riffs: If you have a memorable guitar riff, consider repeating it throughout a section to reinforce its impact. Repetition can make the riff more recognizable and contribute to the overall catchiness of the composition.

Emphasizing Vocal Hooks: If there's a vocal hook in a chorus or verse, experiment with repeating it. Repetition can enhance its memorability and create a strong focal point for the listener.

Building Tension and Release:

Gradual Intensity Building: Experiment with repeating a musical motif, gradually increasing intensity with each repetition. This technique can be especially effective in building tension before a climactic section.

Release Through Repetition: Alternatively, use repetition to create a sense of release. Repeating a melodic or rhythmic pattern can offer a comforting familiarity and a release of tension.

Dynamic Repetition Variations:

Static Repetition: Keep certain sections static with consistent repetition for a hypnotic effect. This can be particularly effective in instrumental breaks or ambient sections.

Evolutionary Repetition: Experiment with variations in repetition, gradually introducing new elements or intensifying existing ones. This dynamic approach keeps the repetition interesting and evolving.

Layering and Texture:

Layered Repetition: Layering repetitive elements, such as multiple guitar tracks playing similar or harmonized parts, can add depth and texture to a section.

Texture Variations: Experiment with changing the texture of repeated elements. For example, start with a clean guitar riff and gradually introduce distortion or other effects with each repetition.

Creating Motifs for Section Identification:

Motif Identification: Establishing a motif through repetition can help identify different sections within the composition. A specific riff or melodic pattern can become a signature element for that section.

Sectional Variation: Experiment with subtly altering the motif each time it repeats in different sections. This variation maintains interest while preserving a sense of cohesion.

Call-and-Response Patterns:

Guitar and Vocal Interaction: Create call-and-response patterns between vocals and guitar. Repetition in this context emphasizes the interaction, creating a dynamic relationship between the guitar and vocals.

Contrasting Repetition: Experiment with contrasting repetition lengths between the vocal and guitar lines. This interplay adds interest and complexity to the overall sound.

Repeating Chord Progressions:

Chord Progression Emphasis: Repeat specific chord progressions to anchor a section. This technique is particularly effective in emphasizing the harmonic structure of the composition.

Chord Variation: Experiment with subtle variations within the repeated chord progression. Introduce inversions, add or remove certain notes, or change the strumming pattern to add nuance.

Repetitive Phrasing for Emphasis:

Lyric Emphasis: Use repetition in lyrics for emphasis. Repeating certain phrases or lines can reinforce the lyrical message and create a strong emotional impact.

Melodic Repetition: Repeat melodic phrases within guitar solos or instrumental sections. This reinforces key musical ideas and provides a sense of unity.

Example:

Consider the intro of Guns N' Roses' *Sweet Child o' Mine*. The iconic guitar riff is repeated, creating a distinctive motif that not only establishes the section but also serves as a recognizable signature throughout the song.

Experimenting with repetition within sections is a versatile tool in guitar composition. It allows you to create familiarity, emphasize key elements, and build dynamic contrasts within your compositions. By thoughtfully incorporating repetition and exploring variations, you can craft engaging and memorable sections that leave a lasting impact on the listener. Trust your creativity and intuition as you experiment with different approaches to repetition in your guitar compositions.

INSTRUMENTAL SECTIONS AND LENGTH

If your composition includes instrumental sections or solos, factor in the appropriate length for these segments. Instrumental sections can vary in length based on their role in the overall composition.

DETERMINING LENGTH OF INSTRUMENTALS

Determining the appropriate lengths of instrumental sections or solos in your guitar composition is a crucial aspect of crafting a well-balanced and engaging song structure.

Narrative:

Contextual Relevance: The length of instrumental sections or solos should align with the narrative and emotional context of the song. Consider the story you're telling or the mood you're conveying and let that guide the duration.

Enhancing Emotional Impact: Longer instrumental sections may be appropriate for building emotional depth, while shorter solos can serve as dynamic bursts of energy.

Listener Interest:

Balancing Act: Strike a balance between holding the listener's interest and avoiding overindulgence. While a captivating guitar solo can be a highlight, excessively long instrumental sections may risk losing the audience's attention.

Dynamic Contrast: Consider the surrounding sections when determining the length of an instrumental part.

Use the instrumental break or solo to provide dynamic contrast within the overall song structure.

Song's Genre:

Genre Norms: Different genres have varying expectations regarding instrumental sections and solos. For example, genres like progressive rock or jazz may allow for more extended instrumental explorations, while pop or punk may favor concise solos.

Genre-Conscious Decision: Be aware of the conventions in the genre you're working within, and decide whether to conform to or challenge those norms based on your artistic vision.

Support the Song's Flow:

Transitional Role: Instrumental sections can serve as effective transitions between different song segments. Consider the role that the instrumental break plays in connecting verses, choruses, or other sections.

Building Momentum: Solos, especially towards the climax of a song, can be used to build momentum. Gauge the song's energy flow and use the solo length to contribute to that buildup.

Expressive and Technical Considerations:

Expressive Intent: The length of a solo may be influenced by the expressive intent. If you're aiming for a soulful, expressive solo, it might be longer to allow for nuanced playing. For technical displays, a shorter, focused solo may be appropriate.

Technical Skill Level: Consider your own technical proficiency as a guitarist. A solo that showcases your strengths without exceeding your capabilities will contribute to a polished and satisfying performance.

Variety and Experimentation:

Dynamic Range: Experiment with dynamic range within the instrumental sections. This can involve variations in intensity, speed, and complexity to keep the listener engaged.

Sectional Variation: If your song includes multiple instrumental sections, experiment with varying their lengths. This adds interest and prevents predictability.

Collaboration and Feedback:

Band Dynamics: If you're working with a band, consider the dynamics and contributions of other instruments. Ensure that instrumental sections complement the overall sound and don't overshadow other elements.

Feedback from Peers: Seek feedback from bandmates, producer, or trusted peers. They can provide valuable perspectives on whether the instrumental sections enhance the song or if adjustments in length are needed.

The appropriate length for instrumental sections or solos in your guitar composition is a subjective decision influenced by various factors, including genre, narrative, and the overall flow of the song. Trust your creative instincts while being mindful of the song's needs. Strive for a balance between expressive freedom and maintaining listener engagement, ensuring that instrumental sections contribute meaningfully to the overall musical experience. Experimentation, feedback, and a deep understanding of your song's context will guide you in determining the most effective lengths for instrumental elements in your guitar composition.

TRANSITIONS AND SECTION LENGTH

Ensure that transitions between sections are seamless and well-paced. The length of a section should support a smooth transition into the next, maintaining the overall coherence of the composition.

ACHIEVING EFFECTIVE TRANSITIONS

Seamless and well-paced transitions between sections is a crucial aspect of crafting a cohesive and engaging song structure in guitar composition. Smooth transitions enhance the flow of the music, maintaining the listener's interest and creating a unified musical journey.

Melodic Continuity:

Connecting Melodies: Create melodic connections between sections. Carry a melodic motif from one section to the next, providing a seamless transition. This could involve using similar phrasing or repeating a melodic sequence.

Example: In The Beatles' *A Day in the Life*, the descending piano chord progression in the bridge smoothly transitions into the next section, creating a sense of continuity.

Harmonic Progression:

Smooth Chord Transitions: Ensure that the harmonic progression in the transition is smooth. Use common chords or pivot chords that naturally link the ending of one section to thc beginning of the next.

Example: The transition between verses and choruses in John Mayer's *Gravity* features a subtle yet effective harmonic progression, contributing to a seamless flow.

Rhythmic Consistency:

Maintaining Rhythmic Patterns: Keep a consistent rhythmic pattern between sections to maintain a sense of continuity. Gradual rhythmic changes can signal a transition without disrupting the overall flow.

Example: The transition between the verse and chorus in Fleetwood Mac's *Go Your Own Way* is characterized by a consistent rhythmic drive, contributing to a smooth flow.

Dynamic Buildup or Release:

Gradual Dynamics: Use dynamic changes to signal transitions. Gradually increase or decrease volume and intensity to build anticipation or provide a sense of release when moving between sections.

Example: The transition from the quiet verses to the explosive chorus in Nirvana's *Smells Like Teen Spirit* employs a dynamic buildup for a powerful impact.

Instrumental Bridges:

Instrumental Interludes: Incorporate short instrumental bridges or interludes between sections. These segments can serve as transitional elements, providing a brief pause before introducing a new musical theme.

Example: The instrumental bridge in Led Zeppelin's *Stairway to Heaven* acts as a transition between the acoustic and electric sections, creating a seamless progression.

Contrasting Elements:

Introduce Contrasting Elements: Experiment with introducing new elements during transitions. This could involve a change in instrumentation, a shift in dynamics, or the introduction of a new rhythmic pattern.

Example: Radiohead's *Paranoid Android* features contrasting elements in its transitions, with shifts in tempo, instrumentation, and vocal delivery, creating a dynamic and unpredictable flow.

Repetition for Cohesion:

Repeating Elements: Repeat certain elements from the preceding section into the transition. This repetition helps bridge the gap between sections and maintains a sense of cohesion.

Example: In U2's *With or Without You*, the sustained guitar note from the verse is repeated in the transition, creating a smooth connection to the chorus.

Tasteful Ornamentation:

Guitar Ornaments: Use tasteful guitar ornaments, such as slides, bends, or arpeggios, in the transition to add subtle embellishments. These nuances can enhance the fluidity between sections.

Example: In Pink Floyd's *Wish You Were Here*, the acoustic guitar solo includes tasteful bends and slides, contributing to the smooth transition between sections.

Drum Fills and Rolls:

Dynamic Drum Elements: Incorporate drum fills or rolls in transitions to create anticipation or provide a rhythmic segue. Well-timed drum fills can signal a change in section.

Example: The transition between sections in Phil Collins' *In the Air Tonight* is marked by an iconic drum fill, adding drama and marking a shift in the song's intensity.

Seamless transitions in guitar composition are achieved through a combination of melodic, harmonic, rhythmic, and dynamic considerations. The key is to maintain a sense of coherence while introducing elements that signal a shift in the musical landscape. Analyze transitions in songs across various genres to gain inspiration and insight into how masterful musicians navigate between sections. Trust your instincts, experiment with different techniques, and seek feedback to refine the transitions in your guitar compositions.

AUDIENCE ATTENTION AND LENGTH

Consider the attention span of your audience. While there are no strict rules, shorter sections might be preferable in genres where listeners have shorter attention spans, while longer, immersive sections may be suitable for certain styles.

ASSESSING AUDIENCE ATTENTION SPANS ACCORDING TO GENRE

Assessing an audience's attention span during a guitar performance is a nuanced task influenced by various factors, including the musical genre, venue, and the preferences of the specific audience. Attention spans can vary widely, and understanding these dynamics is crucial for delivering an engaging performance. While it's challenging to assign specific attention spans to different genres, we can explore general tendencies and considerations.

Classical Music:

Classical music audiences often appreciate longer, intricate compositions. Patrons attending classical concerts tend to be accustomed to extended pieces and have the patience for nuanced performances.

A classical guitarist performing a piece by Bach or Rodrigo may expect the audience to engage with the intricacies and development of the composition over an extended period.

Jazz:

Jazz audiences often appreciate improvisation and longer instrumental solos. The dynamic nature of jazz allows for extended exploration of musical ideas.

In a jazz guitar performance, an extended improvisational section within a standard or during a jazz fusion piece may captivate the audience's attention.

Rock and Pop:

Rock and pop audiences typically enjoy songs with concise structures and catchy hooks. While they may have a preference for shorter tracks, a captivating performance can extend their attention.

A rock guitarist performing a hit song or a well-known guitar solo may capture the audience's attention, but maintaining energy and variety is crucial.

Blues:

Blues audiences appreciate the emotional depth and storytelling within songs. While blues compositions can vary in length, the focus is often on expression and soulful playing.

A blues guitarist delivering a heartfelt solo or playing a traditional blues structure may hold the audience's attention with emotive and evocative playing.

Metal:

Metal audiences are known for their enthusiasm, and they often embrace longer compositions with intricate guitar work. However, maintaining energy is crucial to retain their attention.

In a metal guitar performance, a guitarist showcasing technical prowess in a solo or playing a complex riff may keep the audience engaged.

Folk and Acoustic:

Folk and acoustic audiences appreciate storytelling and often enjoy longer, narrative-driven compositions. They tend to engage well with the intimacy of acoustic performances.

A folk guitarist delivering a ballad or a singer-songwriter performing a reflective acoustic piece may connect with the audience through storytelling.

Electronic and Ambient:

Electronic and ambient music audiences may have a higher tolerance for longer, evolving compositions. The immersive and atmospheric nature of these genres can captivate listeners.

A guitarist incorporating ambient effects and creating sonic landscapes may captivate an audience seeking an immersive experience.

World Music:

World music audiences often embrace diverse rhythms and longer, culturally influenced compositions. The richness of different musical traditions allows for extended exploration.

A guitarist incorporating elements of flamenco, bossa nova, or other world music genres may captivate audiences with the diversity of their playing.

CONSIDERATIONS FOR GAUGING ATTENTION SPAN

Venue:

Concert Halls vs. Clubs: The setting can influence attention spans. Concert halls may encourage longer, focused listening, while clubs may require more immediate engagement.

Audience Expectations:

Fan Base Knowledge: Consider the familiarity of the audience with the music. Well-known songs or genres familiar to the audience may sustain attention more effectively.

Program Variety:

Diversity in Setlist: Incorporate a mix of shorter, impactful pieces and longer, exploratory compositions to cater to different preferences within the audience.

Interactive Elements:

Audience Interaction: Engaging with the audience, sharing anecdotes, or encouraging participation can enhance attention and connection during a performance.

Energy and Dynamics:

Varying Intensity: Maintain a balance of intensity and restraint to keep the performance dynamic. Well-timed peaks and valleys can sustain audience interest.

It's crucial to note that individual preferences within any audience can vary, and the success of a guitar performance often lies in the artist's ability to read the room, adapt to the atmosphere, and deliver a captivating and authentic musical experience. Experimenting with different approaches and observing audience reactions in real-time can provide valuable insights into what works best for a particular context.

BUILDING CONFIDENCE

Ultimately, trust your artistic instincts. If a certain section feels right at a particular length, it likely contributes to the overall emotional and structural integrity of your composition.

TRUST YOUR INSTINCTS

Trusting your artistic instincts in guitar composition is a personal and evolving process. It involves a combination of self-discovery, experimentation, and embracing your unique musical voice.

Here are practical steps to help you build confidence and trust in your artistic instincts when composing for the guitar.

Immerse Yourself in Music:

Diverse Listening: Listen to a broad range of music across various genres. Exposing yourself to different styles will expand your musical palette and influence your compositional approach.

Analyze and Deconstruct Music:

Study Your Favorites: Analyze the music of your favorite guitarists and composers. Understand the structural elements, chord progressions, and techniques they use. This knowledge will empower you to make informed creative choices.

Technical Mastery:

Develop Guitar Skills: Build a solid foundation in guitar technique. Proficiency on the instrument enhances your ability to translate creative ideas into tangible compositions.

Experiment with Different Styles:

Genre Exploration: Don't limit yourself to a single genre. Experiment with various styles and fusion of genres. This experimentation can lead to unique and innovative compositions.

Set a Creative Routine:

Consistent Practice: Establish a regular practice routine for composition. Consistency helps you develop a deeper connection with your instrument and nurtures your creative process.

Embrace Improvisation:

Freestyle Playing: Allow time for improvisation. This unstructured play can unveil spontaneous ideas and help you trust your instincts without the pressure of predefined compositions.

Capture Ideas Promptly:

Recording Device: Keep a recording device or a notebook handy. When inspiration strikes, capture your ideas immediately. This practice prevents creative thoughts from slipping away.

Set Intentions for Your Composition:

Define Goals: Before starting a composition, establish clear intentions. Decide on the mood, theme, or emotion you want to convey. This clarity guides your creative decisions.

Visualize Your Composition:

Mental Imagery: Visualize the sound and atmosphere you want to create. This mental imagery can guide your composition and align your artistic instincts with your vision.

Explore Unconventional Approaches:

Think Outside the Box: Challenge yourself to explore unconventional techniques, tunings, or structures. Pushing boundaries can lead to fresh and unexpected compositions.

Seek Inspiration from Other Art Forms:

Cross-Art Inspiration: Draw inspiration from other art forms like visual arts, literature, or nature. Translating different forms of inspiration into your music adds depth and originality.

Trust Your Emotional Responses:

Connect Emotionally: Pay attention to how your compositions make you feel. Trust your emotional responses as indicators of authentic expression in your music.

Feedback and Reflection:

Solicit Constructive Feedback: Share your compositions with trusted friends, mentors, or fellow musicians. Constructive feedback can provide valuable insights while boosting your confidence.

Celebrate Your Unique Voice:

Individuality Appreciation: Acknowledge and celebrate your unique musical voice. Embracing your individuality fosters confidence in your artistic instincts.

Overcome Perfectionism:

Embrace Imperfections: Accept that not every composition needs to be perfect. Embracing imperfections can lead to more genuine and spontaneous creations.

Evolve and Adapt:

Artistic Growth: Recognize that artistic instincts evolve over time. Allow yourself the freedom to adapt and grow as a musician and composer.

Balance Critique and Self-Expression:

Artistic Balance: Find a balance between constructive critique and self-expression. While external feedback is valuable, trust your inner voice and intuition.

Perform Your Compositions:

Live Engagement: If possible, perform your compositions in front of an audience. The live experience can strengthen your connection to your music and build confidence.

Reflect on Past Achievements:

Progress Acknowledgment: Reflect on your musical journey and acknowledge your progress. Recognizing how far you've come instills confidence in your abilities.

Enjoy the Creative Process:

Fun in Creation: Remember to enjoy the creative process. Let go of expectations and immerse yourself in the joy of making music. Trusting your instincts becomes more natural when it's an enjoyable experience.

Building trust in your artistic instincts is an ongoing and personal journey. Be patient with yourself, stay curious, and approach your compositions with a spirit of exploration. As you continue to refine your skills and express your unique voice, your confidence in trusting your instincts will naturally grow.

Remember that there is no one-size-fits-all approach, and the ideal length for each section is influenced by the unique characteristics of your composition and your creative vision. Balancing repetition, contrast, and narrative progression will guide you toward determining the most effective lengths for the verses, choruses, bridges, and other sections in your guitar composition.

DYNAMICS AND SONG STRUCTURE

Dynamics refer to the varying loudness and intensity of the music. Recognize that dynamics play a crucial role in conveying emotion, building tension, and maintaining listener engagement.

THE ROLE OF DYNAMICS

Dynamics play a crucial role in shaping the emotional landscape and overall impact of a guitar composition. By manipulating the volume, intensity, and energy levels throughout a song, you can create a dynamic journey that captures the listener's attention and conveys a range of emotions. Let's take a closer look at the role of dynamics in song structure for guitar composition.

Building Intensity:

Soft to Loud Dynamics: Gradually increasing the volume and intensity from soft to loud can build anticipation and create a sense of climactic release. This dynamic build-up is effective in transitions from verses to choruses or in the lead-up to a guitar solo.

Example: In Led Zeppelin's *Stairway to Heaven*, the acoustic introduction gradually builds in intensity before erupting into a powerful electric guitar solo.

Creating Contrast Between Sections:

Verse-Chorus Dynamics: Use dynamic contrast between verses and choruses to highlight different sections of the song. Soft verses followed by loud choruses, or vice versa, create a dynamic interplay that keeps the listener engaged.

Example: In Nirvana's *Smells Like Teen Spirit*, the quiet verses contrast sharply with the explosive choruses, contributing to the song's dynamic impact.

Dynamic Variation Within Sections:

Intra-section Dynamics: Vary the dynamics within a section to add nuance and prevent monotony. This could involve subtle volume swells, variations in strumming intensity, or changes in picking dynamics.

Example: Jimi Hendrix's *Little Wing* features dynamic variations within the guitar parts, creating a dynamic ebb and flow within the verses.

Highlighting Instrumental Breaks or Solos:

Dynamics in Solos: Use dynamic changes to emphasize instrumental breaks or guitar solos. Gradual volume swells, dynamic picking, or controlled dynamics can enhance the emotional impact of a solo.

Example: David Gilmour's guitar solo in Pink Floyd's *Comfortably Numb* features nuanced dynamics, contributing to the solo's emotional depth.

Soft and Gentle Phrasing:

Expressive Softness: Soft dynamics can be employed for more delicate and expressive phrasing. This is particularly effective in introspective or melodic sections where a gentler touch is desired.

Example: Eric Clapton's *Tears in Heaven* utilizes soft dynamics to convey a sense of vulnerability and introspection.

Powerful Crescendos:

Crescendo Leading to Climax: Utilize crescendos to gradually increase the volume and intensity, leading to a climactic moment. This is a powerful technique for creating a sense of drama and emotional impact.

Example: The outro of *Layla* by Derek and the Dominos features a crescendo, building to an intense and memorable climax.

Dynamic Control in Fingerpicking:

Fingerpicking Dynamics: In fingerstyle compositions, dynamic control is crucial. Varying the intensity and volume of fingerpicked patterns adds expressiveness and emotional depth.

Example: Fleetwood Mac's *Landslide*, performed by Lindsey Buckingham, showcases intricate fingerpicking dynamics, contributing to the song's intimate atmosphere.

Dynamic Changes in Strumming Patterns:

Strumming Dynamics: Experiment with dynamic changes in strumming patterns. Switching between soft, muted strums and powerful, open strums can create a dynamic contrast within rhythmic sections.

Example: The strumming dynamics in Tracy Chapman's *Fast Car* vary, contributing to the song's dynamic and emotional range.

Effective Use of Silence:

Dramatic Pauses: Silence or near-silence can be a powerful dynamic tool. Introduce brief pauses or silent moments before launching into a powerful section for added impact.

Example: The strategic use of silence in the intro of Metallica's *One* creates a dramatic and attention-grabbing effect.

Dynamic Feedback and Response:

Call and Response Dynamics: Create dynamic interplay between different guitar parts. For instance, a lead guitar line could respond dynamically to rhythmic patterns in the rhythm guitar, enhancing the overall texture.

Example: The call-and-response dynamics between guitar parts in The Eagles' *Hotel California* contribute to the song's intricate and captivating structure.

In guitar composition, dynamics serve as a powerful tool for conveying emotion, shaping the song's structure, and engaging the listener on a visceral level. Whether through subtle variations in volume, explosive crescendos, or delicate fingerpicking, paying attention to dynamics allows you to create a dynamic and captivating musical experience. The examples provided showcase how legendary guitarists have effectively utilized dynamics to elevate their compositions, serving as inspiration for your own explorations in guitar composition.

THE DYNAMIC BLUEPRINT

Create a dynamic blueprint for your composition. Decide where you want peaks and valleys in intensity. For example, choruses often represent peaks, while verses may be more subdued.

CONSIDERATIONS FOR A DYNAMIC BLUEPRINT

Creating a dynamic blueprint for your guitar composition involves strategically planning and organizing the various elements to build tension, release energy, and guide the listener through a compelling musical journey.

Identify Key Sections:

Verses, Choruses, Bridges: Clearly define the key sections of your song, such as verses, choruses, and bridges. Each section serves a specific purpose in advancing the narrative or emotional arc of the composition.

Example: In *Hotel California* by The Eagles, the song follows a structured blueprint with distinct verses, choruses, and instrumental sections, each contributing to the overall dynamic progression.

Determine Dynamic Peaks and Valleys:

Strategic Placement: Identify where you want the dynamic peaks (high-energy moments) and valleys (quieter, more subdued moments) within your composition. This could involve placing climactic guitar solos in specific sections or creating intimate acoustic interludes.

Example: Pink Floyd's *Wish You Were Here* strategically places a powerful guitar solo after a more subdued acoustic section, creating a dynamic contrast.

Establish Transitional Elements:

Smooth Transitions: Plan for transitional elements that seamlessly connect different sections. These could be instrumental bridges, fills, or thematic motifs that provide a smooth transition from one part of the song to another.

Example: The instrumental bridge in Metallica's *Master of Puppets* acts as a transitional element, guiding the listener from a heavy, rhythmic section to a melodic guitar solo.

Experiment with Sectional Lengths:

Varied Section Lengths: Experiment with the lengths of each section to maintain interest. Longer verses followed by shorter, punchy choruses, or vice versa, contribute to a dynamic ebb and flow.

Example: In *Bohemian Rhapsody* by Queen, the song features distinct sections of varying lengths, contributing to its dynamic and unpredictable structure.

Utilize Dynamic Contrast Within Sections:

Intra-section Dynamics: Vary the dynamics within each section to add nuance and prevent monotony. For example, start a verse softly and gradually increase intensity or use dynamic picking to create a sense of movement.

Example: Eric Clapton's *Layla* features dynamic variations within the guitar parts, contributing to the overall expressiveness of the composition.

Experiment with Instrumentation:

Instrumental Diversity: Explore different guitar tones, effects, and techniques to add diversity to your composition. This can involve transitioning from clean to distorted tones or incorporating acoustic and electric elements.

Example: Led Zeppelin's *Whole Lotta Love* showcases dynamic shifts in guitar instrumentation, from Jimmy Page's iconic riff to experimental effects in the instrumental breakdown.

Craft a Climactic Conclusion:

Build to a Climax: Plan for a climactic conclusion to your composition. This could involve a powerful final chorus, an extended guitar solo, or a dramatic instrumental outro that leaves a lasting impression.

Example: Guns N' Roses' *November Rain* builds to a climactic conclusion with an emotive guitar solo and orchestral elements, creating a grand finale.

Consider Tempo and Rhythmic Changes:

Tempo Shifts: Experiment with tempo changes to create dynamic contrast. A subtle acceleration or deceleration can have a significant impact on the overall feel of the composition.

Example: In *Come As You Are* by Nirvana, subtle tempo changes contribute to the song's dynamic shifts between verses and choruses.

Dynamic Feedback and Response Between Instruments:

Guitar Interplay: Plan for dynamic interplay between guitar parts. This could involve call-and-response patterns, harmonized lines, or coordinated dynamic changes between lead and rhythm guitars.

Example: The interplay between lead and rhythm guitars in Metallica's *Fade to Black* creates a dynamic conversation within the composition.

Experiment with Dynamics in Lyrics and Melody:

Lyric Emphasis: Consider how dynamics in vocal delivery can complement guitar dynamics. A softer vocal approach during verses followed by a more powerful delivery in the chorus can enhance the overall dynamic impact.

Example: Pearl Jam's *Alive* features dynamic shifts in both vocal delivery and guitar intensity, creating a dynamic and anthemic quality.

Creating a dynamic blueprint for your guitar composition involves thoughtful planning and experimentation. By strategically organizing sections, transitions, and dynamics, you can craft a composition that engages listeners on an emotional level and takes them on a captivating musical journey. The provided examples illustrate how legendary musicians have effectively applied these concepts in their compositions, serving as inspiration for your own dynamic explorations in guitar composition.

DYNAMIC BLUEPRINT OUTLINE

Creating a dynamic blueprint for structuring a song involves carefully planning the arrangement of various sections to build tension, release energy, and guide the listener through a compelling musical journey.

THE DYNAMIC BLUEPRINT OUTLINE

1.Introduction (0:00 0:30):
-Objective: Capture attention and set the mood for the song.
-Instrumentation: Clean guitar arpeggios, atmospheric effects.
-Dynamics: Soft, gradually building in intensity.

2.Verse 1 (0:30 1:00):
-Objective: Introduce lyrics and melodic themes.
-Instrumentation: Acoustic guitar, light percussion.
-Dynamics: Soft to moderate, allowing room for vocals.

3.Pre-Chorus (1:00 1:15):
-Objective: Build anticipation leading into the chorus.
-Instrumentation: Introduce a subtle increase in dynamics, possibly adding sustained chords or a rising melodic line.

4.Chorus (1:15 1:45):
-Objective: Release energy, introduce a memorable hook.

-Instrumentation: Full band, electric guitars, driving rhythm.

-Dynamics: Moderate to loud, emphasizing the dynamic peak of the song.

5.Instrumental Bridge (1:45 2:15):

-Objective: Transition into a different sonic landscape.

-Instrumentation: Guitar solo, supported by a rhythmic foundation.

-Dynamics: Building intensity, showcasing instrumental prowess.

6.Verse 2 (2:15 2:45):

-Objective: Develop lyrical content, reintroduce earlier themes.

-Instrumentation: Similar to Verse 1 but may include subtle variations.

-Dynamics: Soft to moderate, providing contrast from the chorus.

7.Chorus 2 (2:45 3:15):

-Objective: Reinforce the impact of the chorus.

-Instrumentation: Similar to Chorus 1 but may include additional layers.

-Dynamics: Moderate to loud, maintaining the energy.

8.Bridge (3:15 3:45):

-Objective: Build tension, set the stage for a climactic section.

-Instrumentation: Experiment with dynamic changes, introducing unexpected elements.

-Dynamics: Gradually increasing, creating anticipation.

9.Climax (3:45 4:15):
-Objective: Reach the peak of emotional intensity.

-Instrumentation: Full band, intense guitar solo, powerful vocals.

-Dynamics: Loud, showcasing the highest energy level in the song.

10.Chorus 3 (4:15 4:45):
-Objective: Revisit the chorus, perhaps with slight variations.

-Instrumentation: Similar to previous choruses but may feature additional layers.

-Dynamics: Moderate to loud, providing a familiar yet powerful resolution.

11.Outro (4:45 5:15):
-Objective: Wind down the song, provide closure.

-Instrumentation: Gradually reduce the intensity, possibly returning to clean guitar.

-Dynamics: Soft, gradually fading out.

12.Conclusion (5:15 5:30):
-Objective: Conclude the song and leave a lasting impression.

-Instrumentation: Minimal elements, perhaps a final guitar motif.

-Dynamics: Very soft, creating a sense of finality.

REMEMBER FOR YOUR DYNAMIC BLUEPRINT

Transitions:

Ensure smooth transitions between sections, utilizing techniques like instrumental breaks, fills, or thematic motifs.

Instrumental Variation:

Experiment with different guitar tones, effects, and playing techniques to add variety.

Dynamic Contrast:

Aim for dynamic shifts between sections to maintain listener engagement.

Lyric-Melody Connection:

Align the dynamics of the lyrics with the musical dynamics for a cohesive emotional impact.

This dynamic blueprint serves as a starting point, and you can adapt it based on the specific theme, genre, and emotional tone you intend for your composition. Use these guidelines as a framework and feel free to experiment with variations that suit your creative vision.

GRADUAL BUILDUPS AND STRUCTURE

Use gradual buildups to increase intensity over time. Start with softer dynamics and gradually increase the volume and energy as the composition progresses.

UTILIZING GRADUAL BUILDUPS IN COMPOSITION

Gradual buildups are a powerful tool in guitar composition, allowing you to increase the intensity and energy of a song over time. This technique creates a sense of anticipation and can lead to powerful climaxes or impactful transitions.

Start with Sparse Arrangement:

Initial Section: Begin with a section that features a sparse arrangement, with minimal instrumentation and subdued dynamics.

Example: In *High and Dry* by Radiohead, the song starts with a clean guitar arpeggio and Thom Yorke's vocals, creating a calm and intimate atmosphere.

Gradual Instrumentation Addition:

Buildup Phase 1: Introduce additional instruments gradually, layer by layer. This could involve bringing in a second guitar, bass, or subtle percussion to add complexity.

Example: *Clocks* by Coldplay starts with a simple piano riff, and as the song progresses, more instruments are gradually introduced, building up to a fuller sound.

Dynamic Intensity Increase:

Gradual Dynamics: Increase the intensity of the playing gradually. This can involve playing more aggressively, strumming harder, or using dynamic picking to add intensity.

Example: In *Stairway to Heaven* by Led Zeppelin, the acoustic guitar picking gradually becomes more intense as the song progresses, building towards the iconic guitar solo.

Rhythmic Complexity and Drum Dynamics:

Buildup Phase 2: Introduce rhythmic complexity. Drum patterns can become more intricate, and the guitar can incorporate more complex strumming or picking patterns.

Example: *Black* by Pearl Jam features a gradual buildup in drum intensity and guitar strumming, creating a sense of tension.

Layered Harmonies and Counterpoint:

Buildup Phase 3: Introduce layered harmonies or counterpoint melodies. This adds depth and complexity to the composition, contributing to the overall buildup.

Example: Pink Floyd's *Comfortably Numb* gradually introduces harmonized guitar lines, building up to the climactic guitar solo.

Dynamic Tempo Increase:

Gradual Tempo Acceleration: Consider a gradual increase in tempo to add urgency and excitement. This technique works well in rock and progressive genres.

Example: *Paradise City* by Guns N' Roses gradually increases the tempo as the song progresses, contributing to the energetic buildup.

Use of Crescendos:

Crescendos in Dynamics: Employ crescendos, where the intensity gradually grows louder. This is effective in creating a dramatic and impactful buildup.

Example: The final section of *Layla* by Derek and the Dominos features a crescendo, building to an intense and memorable climax.

Building Towards Guitar Solo:

Guitar Solo as Climax: Consider building the intensity towards a guitar solo. The solo can serve as the pinnacle of the song, showcasing technical prowess and emotional depth.

Example: In *Hotel California* by Eagles, the gradual buildup leads to an iconic guitar solo, serving as a climactic moment in the song.

Vocal Intensity and Range Increase:

Dynamic Vocal Performance: If vocals are present, consider having the singer gradually increase their intensity and vocal range as the song progresses.

Example: Queen's *Bohemian Rhapsody* features Freddie Mercury's vocals gradually intensifying, contributing to the song's dynamic structure.

Culmination in Climactic Section:

Climactic Release: The gradual buildup should lead to a climactic section where all the elements come together, creating a powerful and memorable moment.

Example: *Sweet Child o' Mine* by Guns N' Roses builds up to the iconic guitar riff, creating a climactic release of energy.

Considerations:

Subtle Transitions: Ensure smooth transitions between the buildup phases to maintain a cohesive flow.

Instrumental Dynamics: Experiment with varying guitar tones and effects to enhance the dynamic range.

Genre Sensitivity: Consider the genre conventions and tailor your buildup techniques accordingly.

Using gradual buildups in your guitar composition allows you to control the emotional trajectory of your song, creating a dynamic and engaging listening experience. Analyze how these techniques are employed in various genres and adapt them to suit your creative vision.

CONTRASTS AND STRUCTURE

Create contrasts between different sections. For instance, make sure the chorus is dynamically more powerful than the preceding verse, emphasizing the emotional impact.

CREATING CONTRASTS BETWEEN SECTIONS

Creating contrasts between different sections in a song is essential for maintaining listener engagement and providing a dynamic and interesting musical experience. In guitar composition, these contrasts can be achieved through a combination of various elements.

Dynamics:

Soft vs. Loud: Contrast between quieter, softer sections and louder, more intense sections. This dynamic range creates a sense of tension and release.

Example: The verses in *Smells Like Teen Spirit* by Nirvana are relatively quiet and subdued, providing a stark contrast to the explosive chorus.

Tempo Changes:

Fast vs. Slow: Vary the tempo between sections to create a sense of urgency or relaxation.

Example: In *Stairway to Heaven* by Led Zeppelin, the acoustic intro is slow and contemplative, contrasting with the faster-paced electric guitar-driven sections.

Rhythmic Patterns:

Complex vs. Simple: Utilize intricate and complex rhythmic patterns in one section and simpler, straightforward rhythms in another.

Example: *Black* by Pearl Jam features a complex, palm-muted riff in the verses, contrasting with the open and melodic chorus.

Harmonic Changes:

Harmonic Complexity: Vary the harmonic complexity between sections. Use more intricate chord progressions in one section and simpler ones in another.

Example: Radiohead's *Paranoid Android* features sections with complex, dissonant chords contrasted with more straightforward chord progressions.

Instrumentation:

Full Band vs. Stripped Down: Change the instrumentation between sections. Transition from a full band sound to a stripped-down arrangement or vice versa.

Example: In *The Chain* by Fleetwood Mac, the verses are driven by a stripped-down guitar and vocal arrangement, while the chorus introduces a fuller band sound.

Texture Variation:

Thick vs. Thin Texture: Alter the overall texture of the arrangement. Move from sections with a thick, layered sound to sections with a more transparent and open texture.

Example: *November Rain* by Guns N' Roses features contrasting sections with dense orchestration and quieter, more intimate moments.

Melodic Variation:

Melodic Complexity: Vary the melodic complexity between sections. Have sections with intricate and elaborate melodies followed by simpler, more straightforward melodic lines.

Example: In *Sweet Child o' Mine* by Guns N' Roses, the verses feature a relatively simple melody, while the guitar solo introduces a more intricate and expressive melodic line.

Harmony and Modulation:

Key Changes: Introduce key changes or modulations between sections to create a sense of movement and contrast.

Example: *Bohemian Rhapsody* by Queen features distinct sections with different keys, contributing to the song's dynamic structure.

Lyric and Vocal Delivery:

Vocal Intensity: Vary vocal delivery and intensity between sections. Move from soft, intimate singing to powerful, emotive vocals.

Example: Pearl Jam's *Alive* features contrasting sections with Eddie Vedder's subdued vocals in the verses and more intense, powerful singing in the choruses.

Riff vs. Chord Progression:

Riff-based vs. Chord-based: Alternate between riff-based sections and chord progression-driven sections to diversify the sonic landscape.

Example: *Smoke on the Water* by Deep Purple contrasts a famous guitar riff with simpler chord-based sections.

Rhythmic Feel:

Change in Time Signatures: Experiment with changing time signatures to alter the rhythmic feel between sections.

Example: Tool's *Schism* features sections with different time signatures, contributing to the song's rhythmic complexity.

Lyric Theme:

Contrasting Themes: If applicable, vary the lyrical theme or mood between sections. This can add an additional layer of contrast.

Example: In Pink Floyd's *Wish You Were Here*, the lyrics in the acoustic verses contrast with the more abstract and introspective themes in the instrumental sections.

Considerations:

Smooth Transitions: Ensure transitions between contrasting sections are smooth to maintain overall cohesion.

Emotional Arc: Consider the emotional arc of the song and how each section contributes to the overall narrative or mood.

Genre Influences: Be aware of genre conventions and expectations, adapting contrasts to suit the style of music you are creating.

By consciously incorporating contrasts between different sections in your guitar composition, you can create a dynamic and compelling musical journey for the listener. Analyze how these techniques are employed in your favorite songs across genres and use them as inspiration for crafting your own unique sonic palette.

CREATING CONTRAST WITHIN SECTIONS

Introduce dynamic contrast within individual sections. Within a verse, for example, experiment with softer and louder phrases to maintain interest.

Dynamic contrast within individual sections of a song is a crucial element in keeping the listener engaged and creating a sense of musical depth and complexity. In guitar composition, this involves varying the intensity, volume, and emotional impact within a specific section.

Varying Guitar Dynamics:

Soft vs. Loud Picking: Experiment with picking dynamics. Start a section softly and gradually increase the picking intensity or vice versa.

Example: Jimi Hendrix's *Little Wing* features sections where the guitar dynamics shift from soft, delicate picking to more aggressive strumming.

Playing Techniques:

Contrasting Techniques: Incorporate different playing techniques within a section. Switch between fingerpicking, palm-muted strumming, and power chords to add variety.

Example: In Metallica's *Fade to Black*, the verses utilize clean arpeggios, while the choruses introduce power chords and distorted strumming for dynamic contrast.

Utilize Guitar Effects:

Clean vs. Distorted Tones: Experiment with clean and distorted guitar tones within a section. This can create a stark contrast in sonic textures.

Example: In *Wish You Were Here* by Pink Floyd, the clean acoustic guitar sections contrast with the distorted electric guitar segments, contributing to the song's dynamic range.

Rhythmic Variations:

Changing Strumming Patterns: Alter strumming patterns within a section. Switch between steady strumming, arpeggios, and syncopated rhythms for dynamic interest.

Example: Tracy Chapman's *Fast Car* features rhythmic variations in the guitar strumming patterns throughout the verses, contributing to the song's dynamic feel.

Volume Swells:

Gradual Volume Changes: Use volume swells to create dynamic shifts within a section. Gradually increasing or decreasing the volume adds a subtle yet effective contrast.

Example: The Edge of U2 often employs volume swells in guitar sections, creating a smooth and dynamic transition between chords.

Picking Intensity:

Soft Fingerpicking vs. Hard Strumming: Contrast between soft fingerpicking and hard strumming. This variation in picking intensity can convey different emotions.

Example: In *Tears in Heaven* by Eric Clapton, the softer fingerpicked sections contrast with the emotionally charged strumming in other parts of the song.

Emphasize Note Dynamics:

Accentuated Notes: Emphasize certain notes within a section. This can be achieved through techniques like hammer-ons, pull-offs, or slides.

Example: Stevie Ray Vaughan's *Texas Flood* features dynamic contrasts achieved through accentuated notes and expressive slides.

Percussive Elements:

Incorporate Percussive Hits: Introduce percussive hits on the guitar body or strings to create rhythmic accents and dynamic contrast.

Example: John Mayer incorporates percussive hits in songs like *Heart of Life*, adding a rhythmic element and dynamic diversity to the guitar playing.

Guitar Solos:

Buildup in Solos: If a section includes a guitar solo, create dynamic contrast within the solo itself. Start with subtle, melodic phrases and gradually build up to more intense and technical passages.

Example: David Gilmour's guitar solo in Pink Floyd's *Comfortably Numb* is a masterclass in creating dynamic contrast within a solo.

Harmonic Variations:

Contrasting Harmonic Elements: Experiment with harmonic variations within a section. Shift between major and minor chords, or introduce unexpected chord changes for dynamic impact.

Example: The Beatles' *A Hard Day's Night* features dynamic harmonic variations, with the verses characterized by major chords and the bridge introducing minor chords.

Considerations:

Serve the Song's Emotion: Ensure that dynamic contrast enhances the emotional impact of the section and serves the overall mood of the song.

Transitional Phrases: Use transitional phrases to smoothly connect contrasting elements, avoiding abrupt shifts that may disrupt the flow.

Listen Critically: Analyze how dynamic contrast is employed in songs across different genres, paying attention to the specific techniques used in guitar composition.

Dynamic contrast within individual sections adds nuance and excitement to your guitar composition. By leveraging various playing techniques, tones, and rhythmic elements, you can create a rich and engaging sonic landscape that captivates the listener throughout the song.

CRESCENDOS AND DECRESCENDOS

Incorporate crescendos (gradual increase in volume) and decrescendos (gradual decrease in volume) to shape phrases and sections dynamically.

INCORPORATING CRESCENDOS AND DECRESCENDOS

Utilizing crescendos and decrescendos in guitar composition is a powerful way to add dramatic intensity, emotional impact, and dynamic contrast to your music. Crescendos involve a gradual increase in volume and intensity, while decrescendos involve a gradual decrease.

Building Intensity with Crescendos:

Instrumentation Gradually Intensifies: Start with a softer dynamic level and gradually increase the intensity by adding more instruments or playing with greater force.

Example: Pink Floyd's *Comfortably Numb* builds intensity through a guitar solo, with David Gilmour gradually increasing both volume and emotional expression.

Layered Crescendos:

Add Layers of Sound: Introduce new layers of sound as the crescendo progresses, creating a more complex and immersive sonic experience.

Example: Explosions in the Sky's *Your Hand in Mine* features layered crescendos, gradually building from minimal guitar melodies to a full, orchestral climax.

Dynamic Strumming/Picking Patterns:

Increase Strumming or Picking Intensity: As the section progresses, gradually shift from gentler strumming or picking patterns to more intense and powerful techniques.

Example: Mumford & Sons' *I Will Wait* incorporates a crescendo effect through the gradual intensification of strumming patterns.

Harmonic Intensification:

Shift to Higher Harmonic Intensity: Gradually introduce higher or more complex harmonics to elevate the emotional intensity of the composition.

Example: Explosions in the Sky's *The Birth and Death of the Day* uses harmonic intensification to build towards a powerful climax.

Tempo Acceleration:

Gradual Tempo Increase: Increase the tempo gradually to add a sense of urgency and excitement to the crescendo.

Example: The crescendo in Metallica's *One* is accompanied by a gradual increase in tempo, heightening the overall intensity of the section.

Lead Guitar Buildup:

Guitar Solo or Lead Buildup: If applicable, use a lead guitar solo or melodic buildup as a focal point for the crescendo, creating a sense of climax.

Example: Guns N' Roses' *November Rain* features a guitar solo by Slash that builds in intensity, contributing to the overall crescendo effect.

Voice Leading:

Melodic Ascension: Utilize melodic lines that ascend gradually, contributing to the upward trajectory of the crescendo.

Example: The guitar solo in Joe Satriani's *Always with Me, Always with You* features melodic lines that ascend, creating a sense of dynamic growth.

Crescendo into Chorus:

Lead into Chorus Intensity: Use a crescendo as a build-up that leads directly into a chorus, amplifying the impact of the chorus.

Example: U2's *Where the Streets Have No Name* builds with a crescendo into the chorus, creating a powerful and anthemic effect.

Decrescendos for Contrast:

Gradual Decrease in Intensity: Create contrast by introducing decrescendos after intense sections, allowing for a gentle release of tension.

Example: The Beatles' *A Day in the Life* features a decrescendo after the climactic orchestral section, transitioning into a more subdued outro.

Strategic Placement:

Strategically Positioned Crescendos: Place crescendos at key moments in the song, such as leading into a bridge, solo, or the final chorus, for maximum impact.

Example: Explosions in the Sky's *The Only Moment We Were Alone* features crescendos strategically positioned throughout the song, creating peaks of emotional intensity.

Considerations:

Serve the Song's Narrative: Ensure that the use of crescendos and decrescendos aligns with the emotional narrative and structure of your composition.

Smooth Transitions: Pay attention to transitions between sections to maintain coherence as you shift dynamics.

Experiment with Texture: Use crescendos to build up the texture of the arrangement, adding layers gradually for a richer sound.

By incorporating crescendos and decrescendos into your guitar composition, you can evoke powerful emotions, create engaging climaxes, and guide listeners through a dynamic musical journey. Experiment with these techniques to find the right balance for your desired emotional impact and overall song structure.

ARTICULATION TECHNIQUES

Experiment with different articulation techniques, such as staccato and legato playing. Varying articulation contributes to dynamic expression.

ARTICULATION AND DYNAMIC EXPRESSION

Articulation techniques in guitar composition play a crucial role in shaping the dynamic expression, adding nuance, and conveying emotion in your music. These techniques involve manipulating how notes are played, contributing to the overall texture and feel of a piece.

Legato:

Definition: Legato involves playing notes smoothly, with minimal separation between them.

Contribution to Dynamic Expression: Legato creates a flowing and connected sound, contributing to a smooth and expressive feel.

Example: A legato passage in a melodic line might involve hammer-ons and pull-offs between notes rather than picking each one individually.

Staccato:

Definition: Staccato is characterized by playing notes in a short and detached manner, with brief pauses between them.

Contribution to Dynamic Expression: Staccato adds a percussive quality to the music, creating a sense of urgency or crispness.

Example: Playing a short and punctuated chord progression with quick, muted strums can introduce a staccato feel.

Hammer-Ons and Pull-Offs:

Definition: Hammer-ons involve picking a note and then tapping a finger onto a higher fret to produce another note. Pull-offs involve plucking a note and then quickly removing the finger to reveal a lower note.

Contribution to Dynamic Expression: These techniques enhance legato playing, allowing for smooth transitions between notes and enabling faster and more fluid passages.

Example: In a solo, incorporating hammer-ons and pull-offs between notes can create a sense of continuity and expressiveness.

Slides:

Definition: Slides involve smoothly transitioning between two or more notes by sliding the fretting hand along the strings.

Contribution to Dynamic Expression: Slides introduce a gliding effect, adding a sense of fluidity and connecting distinct pitches.

Example: A slide from a lower to a higher note in a melody can evoke a sense of upward movement and heightened emotion.

Bends:

Definition: Bending a note involves pushing or pulling a string to change its pitch, creating a gradual increase or decrease in pitch.

Contribution to Dynamic Expression: Bends add emotion and intensity to the sound, allowing for expressive pitch variations.

Example: A well-placed bend in a guitar solo can convey emotion, such as a bending note reaching a higher pitch for added intensity.

Vibrato:

Definition: Vibrato is achieved by oscillating the pitch of a note rapidly, usually through small movements of the fretting hand.

Contribution to Dynamic Expression: Vibrato adds warmth and character to sustained notes, enhancing expressiveness.

Example: Applying vibrato to a sustained note in a lead guitar line can infuse the melody with a more emotive quality.

Palm Muting:

Definition: Palm muting involves resting the palm lightly on the strings near the bridge while playing, resulting in a muted and percussive sound.

Contribution to Dynamic Expression: Palm muting adds a percussive, controlled quality, suitable for creating dynamics in rhythm guitar parts.

Example: Palm muting the verses of a song and then opening up the strings for a more resonant sound in the chorus can create a dynamic contrast.

Tremolo Picking:

Definition: Tremolo picking is rapidly picking a single note or alternating between two notes, creating a shimmering effect.

Contribution to Dynamic Expression: Tremolo picking adds intensity and energy, especially in faster-paced sections.

Example: Using tremolo picking during a climactic section of a composition can heighten the overall dynamic impact.

Harmonics:

Definition: Harmonics involve lightly touching the strings at specific nodes to produce bell-like tones.

Contribution to Dynamic Expression: Harmonics can add ethereal or sparkling textures, contributing to a diverse sonic palette.

Example: Introducing harmonics in a clean guitar passage or during a transition can create a unique dynamic contrast.

Bass Note Emphasis:

Definition: Emphasizing certain bass notes within chords or arpeggios to create a melodic or rhythmic focus.

Contribution to Dynamic Expression: Shifting the emphasis to specific bass notes can provide a sense of movement and drive.

Example: In a fingerstyle arrangement, emphasizing the bass notes in a chord progression can create a dynamic foundation.

Dynamic Picking:

Definition: Varying the intensity of picking strokes, incorporating picking dynamics to control the volume.

Contribution to Dynamic Expression: Dynamic picking adds nuances in volume, contributing to the overall dynamic range of the composition.

Example: Using soft picking for an intimate section and then transitioning to aggressive picking for a powerful climax.

Experimenting with these articulation techniques and combining them thoughtfully in your guitar composition can greatly enhance the expressiveness and dynamic range of your music. As you incorporate these techniques, pay attention to how they interact with each other and contribute to the overall emotional impact of your composition.

DYNAMICS AND MELODIC PHRASING

Use dynamics to highlight specific melodic phrases. Bring out important themes or motifs by emphasizing them with changes in volume.

EXPERIMENTING WITH TEMPO CHANGES

Experimenting with tempo changes in guitar composition is a compelling way to introduce layers of dynamic variation, adding depth and complexity to your music. Temporal shifts can influence the overall feel, energy, and emotional impact of a song.

Gradual Tempo Acceleration:

Building Energy: Start a section at a moderate tempo and gradually accelerate, building energy and intensity.

Example: *Baba O'Riley* by The Who features a gradual tempo acceleration, creating a sense of excitement leading into the energetic sections.

Tempo Deceleration for Emphasis:

Highlighting Emotional Moments: Slow down the tempo for emotional emphasis, allowing listeners to fully absorb and connect with poignant lyrics or instrumental passages.

Example: In Eric Clapton's *Tears in Heaven*, the tempo slows down during the instrumental sections, accentuating the emotional impact.

Shifts Between Verses and Choruses:

Contrast Between Sections: Experiment with different tempos for verses and choruses, creating a clear contrast in energy levels.

Example: Nirvana's *Smells Like Teen Spirit* employs a faster tempo in the chorus, contributing to the dynamic shift from the slower verses.

Tempo Rubato (Free Tempo):

Expressive Phrasing: Introduce moments of rubato, where the tempo becomes more flexible. This adds expressive phrasing, allowing for subtle accelerations and decelerations.

Example: Jazz guitarist Joe Pass often used rubato in his solo performances, showcasing the expressive potential of free tempo.

Tempo Mapping for Narrative Arc:

Align with Song's Storyline: Use tempo changes to reflect the narrative arc of your composition. Accelerate during climactic moments and decelerate for introspective or contemplative sections.

Example: *Bohemian Rhapsody* by Queen features dynamic tempo changes that align with the song's dramatic storyline.

Syncopated Rhythms at Different Tempos:

Layered Rhythmic Complexity: Overlay syncopated rhythms at different tempos, creating layers of rhythmic complexity and interest.

Example: Tool's *Schism* incorporates complex, syncopated rhythms at various tempos, contributing to the intricate feel of the composition.

Rubato Transitions Between Sections:

Smooth Transitions: Use rubato transitions to smoothly shift between sections with distinct tempos, avoiding abrupt changes.

Example: In Led Zeppelin's *Kashmir*, rubato transitions help seamlessly connect sections with different tempos, contributing to the song's epic feel.

Polyrhythmic Experimentation:

Layering Different Rhythms: Experiment with polyrhythms at varying tempos, creating an intricate sonic landscape with overlapping rhythms.

Example: Animals as Leaders, a progressive metal band, often uses polyrhythmic patterns at different tempos to achieve a complex and dynamic sound.

Tempo Changes for Transitions:

Enhancing Section Transitions: Use tempo changes as transitional elements, guiding the listener smoothly from one section to another.

Example: Pink Floyd's *Time* features tempo changes that enhance the transitions between the verses and the instrumental sections.

Tempo Shifts in Instrumental Breaks:

Expressive Instrumentation: Incorporate tempo shifts during instrumental breaks or solos to add expressiveness and dynamic variation.

Example: Joe Satriani's *Surfing with the Alien* features tempo shifts during the guitar solo, enhancing the overall intensity.

Considerations:

Metronome Markings: Be precise with metronome markings to communicate tempo changes effectively.

Experiment with Subtle Changes: Small, subtle tempo changes can have a significant impact on the overall feel of the composition.

Practice Dynamics: Experimenting with tempo changes may require practice to ensure seamless transitions and maintain musicality.

By experimenting with tempo changes, you can create a dynamic and engaging musical experience in your guitar compositions. These variations add layers of interest, emphasize emotional moments, and contribute to the overall dynamic structure of your music. Take inspiration from various genres and adapt these techniques to suit your creative vision.

CONTRAST BETWEEN INSTRUMENTS

If your composition includes multiple instruments, create dynamic contrast between them. For example, let a guitar solo be dynamically distinct from the accompanying chords.

CREATE DYNAMIC CONTRAST BETWEEN INSTRUMENTS

Dynamic contrast between instruments is a key aspect of creating an interesting and compelling song structure in guitar composition. By varying the dynamics, timbres, and roles of different instruments, you can add layers of texture and emotion to your music.

Instrument Selection:

Diverse Instrument Palette: Choose a mix of instruments that complement each other but have distinct sonic characteristics. This could include guitars, bass, drums, keyboards, and other instruments.

Example: The Eagles' *Hotel California* combines acoustic and electric guitars, layered vocals, and a prominent lead guitar, creating a rich and diverse sonic palette.

Dynamic Range:

Utilize Full Dynamic Range: Allow each instrument to occupy a specific dynamic range, from soft and subtle to loud and powerful. This adds depth and contrast to the overall sound.

Example: In Fleetwood Mac's *The Chain*, the bass and drums provide a strong foundation in the lower dynamic range, while the vocals and guitars add intensity in the mid-to-high range.

Instrument Roles:

Varying Instrument Roles: Experiment with assigning different roles to instruments across sections. For example, have the guitar take on a lead role in one section and a rhythmic role in another.

Example: Metallica's *Master of Puppets* features sections where the guitar alternates between aggressive riffing and melodic lead lines, showcasing varied roles.

Instrument Solos:

Feature Instrumental Solos: Allow different instruments to take the spotlight with solos. This creates moments of focused attention and contributes to the overall dynamic structure.

Example: In Dire Straits' *Sultans of Swing*, the guitar solo serves as a focal point, contrasting with the rest of the instrumentation.

Textural Contrasts:

Create Textural Variation: Change the texture by introducing or removing instruments in different sections. This can create a sense of movement and development.

Example: Radiohead's *Karma Police* features sections with sparse instrumentation, allowing the vocals and acoustic guitar to stand out, followed by fuller sections with additional instrumentation.

Dynamic Panning:

Spatial Arrangement: Experiment with panning instruments across the stereo spectrum to create a sense of space. This can enhance the listener's experience and contribute to dynamic contrast.

Example: Pink Floyd's *Money* uses dynamic panning to move the sound of cash registers around the stereo field, creating an immersive effect.

Instrumentation Changes:

Sectional Instrumentation Variations: Change the instrumentation between sections to keep the sound fresh and dynamic. Consider introducing new instruments or removing some for contrast.

Example: The Beatles' *A Day in the Life* features a transition from a sparse, piano-based section to a full orchestral arrangement, creating a dramatic shift in instrumentation.

Contrasting Playing Techniques:

Diverse Playing Techniques: Encourage instruments to use a variety of playing techniques. For instance, contrast between fingerpicking and strumming on the guitar or between different drumming styles.

Example: Led Zeppelin's *Whole Lotta Love* showcases dynamic contrast with Jimmy Page's iconic guitar riff, transitioning to quieter, more experimental sections.

Instrumental Breaks:

Dynamic Instrumental Breaks: Insert instrumental breaks where instruments can showcase their capabilities. These breaks can serve as a dynamic focal point within the song.

Example: The instrumental break in Queen's *Bohemian Rhapsody* features dynamic contrasts between piano, guitar, and vocal harmonies.

Rhythmic Variations:

Varying Rhythmic Patterns: Experiment with different rhythmic patterns across instruments to create rhythmic contrasts, adding complexity and interest.

Example: Santana's *Smooth* incorporates dynamic rhythm guitar patterns alongside Carlos Santana's lead guitar lines, creating a rhythmic and melodic interplay.

Considerations:

Arrangement Cohesion: Ensure that the diverse instrumentation and dynamics contribute to a cohesive and unified sound.

Frequency Spectrum: Be mindful of the frequency spectrum each instrument occupies, allowing space for all elements to be heard distinctly.

Purposeful Changes: Make instrumentational changes purposeful, contributing to the overall emotional arc and narrative of the song.

By consciously considering the dynamic interplay between instruments in your guitar composition, you can create a rich, engaging, and multi-dimensional sonic experience. Experiment with these techniques, analyze the works of artists across genres, and adapt these concepts to suit your unique creative vision.

INSTRUMENTAL TECHNIQUES AND DYNAMICS

If your composition involves specific instrumental techniques (e.g., fingerpicking, hammer-ons, slides), use dynamics to enhance the expressiveness of these techniques.

UTILIZING DYNAMICS ON INSTRUMENTAL TECHNIQUES

Using dynamics to enhance the expressiveness of fingerpicking, hammer-ons, and slides is a powerful technique in guitar composition. These techniques, when executed with varying degrees of force and subtlety, can add nuance, emotion, and a dynamic range to your playing.

Fingerpicking Dynamics:
Soft vs. Firm Picking: Experiment with the dynamics of your fingerpicking. Soft, delicate picking can create a gentle, intimate atmosphere, while firmer picking adds intensity.

Example: The fingerpicking in *Blackbird* by The Beatles showcases dynamic contrast, with softer picking in the verses and a more robust approach in the instrumental sections.

Hammer-Ons with Varying Intensity:
Gradual Hammer-Ons: Use hammer-ons to introduce notes with a gradual increase in intensity. This can create a sense of building energy or emotion.

Example: In Eric Clapton's *Tears in Heaven*, the hammer-ons in the acoustic guitar solo contribute to the song's emotional depth.

Slides with Dynamic Variation:

Slide Intensity: Vary the speed and intensity of slides. Slower, controlled slides can evoke a different emotion than quick and energetic slides.

Example: The iconic opening riff of Led Zeppelin's *Whole Lotta Love* features dynamic slides that contribute to the song's powerful and dynamic feel.

Combining Techniques for Contrast:

Mixing Fingerpicking with Slides and Hammer-Ons: Integrate different techniques within a passage for added expressiveness. Transition between fingerpicking, slides, and hammer-ons to create contrasts.

Example: *Dust in the Wind* by Kansas combines fingerpicking with hammer-ons, creating a dynamic and expressive acoustic guitar arrangement.

Dynamic Phrasing in Solo Sections:

Expressive Soloing: When incorporating fingerpicking, slides, and hammer-ons in a solo section, focus on dynamic phrasing. Emphasize certain notes with varying degrees of intensity.

Example: Mark Knopfler's solo in Dire Straits' *Sultans of Swing* utilizes fingerpicking and dynamic slides for a highly expressive and melodic sound.

Contrast in Verse and Chorus:

Dynamics Between Sections: Use dynamics to distinguish between verse and chorus sections. For example, employ softer fingerpicking in the verses and more forceful strumming or sliding in the choruses.

Example: Bob Dylan's *Don't Think Twice, It's All Right* features subtle fingerpicking in the verses and more pronounced strumming in the chorus.

Crescendos with Fingerpicking:

Gradual Volume Buildup: Build up volume gradually in a section using fingerpicking. This can lead to a crescendo, intensifying the emotional impact.

Example: *Dust in the Wind* builds dynamics through a fingerpicked arpeggio pattern, creating a crescendo effect.

Expressive Slides in Chord Progressions:

Slides within Chords: Incorporate slides within chord progressions to add expressiveness. Experiment with different slide lengths for varying effects.

Example: The Eagles' *Take It to the Limit* features expressive slides within chords, enhancing the emotional delivery of the song.

Gradual Release of Tension:

Controlled Release in Slides and Hammer-Ons: Use slides and hammer-ons to release tension gradually. This technique is effective in creating a sense of resolution.

Example: In *Landslide* by Fleetwood Mac, Lindsey Buckingham's guitar work includes slides and hammer-ons that contribute to the song's introspective mood.

Dynamic Fingerpicking Patterns:

Varying Fingerpicking Patterns: Experiment with different fingerpicking patterns, adjusting the intensity based on the emotional context of the song.

Example: Simon & Garfunkel's *The Sound of Silence* features dynamic fingerpicking patterns that enhance the melancholic atmosphere.

Considerations:

Serve the Song: Ensure that the dynamic choices enhance the overall emotional tone and narrative of the song.

Controlled Technique: Maintain control over your playing technique to execute dynamics with precision.

Use of Silence: Integrate moments of silence or softer passages between dynamic sections to accentuate the impact.

By consciously incorporating dynamics into your fingerpicking, hammer-ons, and slides, you can elevate the expressiveness of your guitar composition. Experiment with these techniques, paying attention to how variations in intensity can convey different emotions and contribute to the overall dynamic structure of your music.

MUTED STRUMS AND PICKING PATTERNS

Integrate muted strums and picking patterns for dynamic variation. These techniques can create percussive and dynamic elements within your playing.

EXPERIMENTING WITH STRUMS AND PICKING

Experimenting with muted strums and picking patterns is an excellent way to introduce dynamic variations and rhythmic interest in your guitar compositions. Muted strums, often achieved through palm muting, and diverse picking patterns can add texture, percussive elements, and dynamic contrast to your playing.

Palm Muting for Muted Strums:

Define Percussive Rhythms: Use palm muting to create muted strums that provide a percussive and rhythmic foundation. This technique is effective for introducing a driving rhythm in certain sections.

Example: Metallica's *Enter Sandman* employs palm-muted strums to create a distinctive and rhythmic main riff.

Dynamics Through Muted Strumming:

Varying Palm Pressure: Experiment with varying palm pressure during muted strums to achieve dynamic contrast. Lighter palm pressure can result in softer muted strums, while firmer pressure produces a more pronounced percussive effect.

Example: John Mayer's *Gravity* features sections with dynamically controlled muted strums, enhancing the overall feel of the song.

Muted Picking Patterns:

Incorporate Muted Notes in Picking Patterns: Integrate muted notes within picking patterns to add complexity and a sense of syncopation. Combine open strings with muted strums for dynamic contrast.

Example: Andy McKee's *Drifting* showcases muted picking patterns that create intricate rhythmic textures on the acoustic guitar.

Strumming Intensity Variations:

Gradual Buildup in Intensity: Experiment with gradually increasing the intensity of muted strums to build tension and energy within a section. This can lead to impactful transitions.

Example: In Dave Matthews Band's *Crash Into Me*, the intensity of palm-muted strums gradually builds throughout the song, contributing to its emotional impact.

Chord Stabs with Muted Strums:

Dynamic Chord Stabs: Use chord stabs with muted strums to create a punchy and dynamic effect. This technique is effective in accentuating specific beats or accents.

Example: In The White Stripes' *Seven Nation Army*, the iconic guitar riff features dynamic chord stabs with palm muting, creating a memorable and rhythmic motif.

Combining Muted and Open Strums:

Contrast Between Muted and Open Strums: Alternate between muted and open strums to introduce dynamic variation. This can create a call-and-response effect within your playing.

Example: *Wish You Were Here* by Pink Floyd combines open strums with muted strums, contributing to the song's distinctive sound.

Percussive Picking Patterns:

Accentuating Percussive Elements: Integrate percussive picking patterns that involve both muted and open strings. This can add a rhythmic and percussive layer to your guitar playing.

Example: Newton Faulkner's *Dream Catch Me* features dynamic picking patterns that incorporate muted and open strings, creating a lively and rhythmic feel.

Muted Strums in Chorus Buildups:

Building Tension in Choruses: Use muted strums to build tension leading into choruses or climactic sections. This can be achieved by gradually increasing the intensity and speed of the muted strums.

Example: In Green Day's *Boulevard of Broken Dreams*, muted strums are employed to build tension before the powerful chorus kicks in.

Syncopated Muted Patterns:

Explore Syncopation: Experiment with syncopated muted patterns to introduce unexpected accents and create rhythmic interest. This adds a layer of complexity to your playing.

Example: John Butler's *Ocean* incorporates syncopated muted patterns, showcasing intricate and dynamic guitar work.

Muted Strums in Bridge Sections:

Textural Changes in Bridges: Use muted strums to create a change in texture during bridge sections. This can provide a sonic contrast and maintain listener engagement.

Example: Incubus' *Drive* utilizes muted strums in the bridge to introduce a different texture before returning to the main riff.

Considerations:

Precision in Palm Muting: Maintain precision in your palm muting technique to control the balance between muted and open sounds.

Experiment with Pick Thickness: The thickness of your guitar pick can influence the dynamics of muted strums. Experiment with different pick types to find the one that suits your desired sound.

Use of Rests: Integrate rests and pauses between muted strums for rhythmic clarity and to create a sense of space.

Experimenting with muted strums and picking patterns provides a versatile toolkit for enhancing the rhythmic and dynamic aspects of your guitar compositions. These techniques can be applied across various genres to add flair, expressiveness, and rhythmic complexity to your playing.

SILENCE AND PAUSES

Embrace moments of silence or pauses for dramatic effect. A sudden drop in volume can be as impactful as a loud crescendo.

LEVERAGING SILENCE AND PAUSES

Silence or pauses, often referred to as "rests," are powerful tools in guitar composition for creating dramatic effects and enhancing dynamics. The strategic use of silence can build tension, emphasize certain moments, and contribute to the overall ebb and flow of your song structure.

Creating Anticipation:

Strategic Pauses: Introduce intentional pauses before a significant change in the song, such as a chorus, solo, or dynamic shift. This creates anticipation and captures the listener's attention.

Example: Radiohead's *Creep* utilizes a brief pause before the explosive chorus, heightening the impact of the dynamic change.

Emphasizing Transition Points:

Pause Between Sections: Use a brief silence to mark the transition between song sections. This can signal a shift in dynamics, mood, or intensity.

Example: The Beatles' *A Day in the Life* features a distinct pause between the somber verses and the orchestral climax, emphasizing the transition.

Dynamic Release:

Silence Before a Release: Incorporate a short pause before a powerful strum or chord progression. This brief silence emphasizes the subsequent release of energy.

Example: In Nirvana's *Smells Like Teen Spirit*, a momentary pause before the loud chorus contributes to the song's dynamic impact.

Building Tension:

Extended Pauses for Tension: Experiment with longer pauses to build tension. This can be particularly effective before a climactic moment in the song.

Example: Pink Floyd's *Wish You Were Here* features extended pauses, creating tension before the emotive guitar solos.

Percussive Breaks:

Silent Percussive Hits: Use silence to punctuate percussive hits or stops, creating a staccato effect. This technique adds a rhythmic dynamic to your playing.

Example: In Led Zeppelin's *Whole Lotta Love*, the band incorporates brief silences between guitar riffs, contributing to the song's dynamic and rhythmic complexity.

Expressive Intervals:

Pause for Emotional Impact: Insert moments of silence after emotionally charged lyrics or instrumental passages. This allows the listener to absorb and reflect on the preceding content.

Example: Leonard Cohen's *Hallelujah* uses pauses after poignant phrases, enhancing the emotional impact of the song.

Strategic Rests in Instrumentals:

Silent Breaks in Solos: Introduce brief rests within guitar solos to add drama and accentuate specific phrases. This allows for dynamic contrast within instrumental sections.

Example: Joe Satriani's *Always with Me, Always with You* includes strategic rests in the guitar solo, contributing to its expressive and dynamic nature.

Surprising Breaks:

Unexpected Pauses: Incorporate unexpected pauses to surprise and engage the listener. This can be particularly effective in unconventional song structures.

Example: The White Stripes' *Seven Nation Army* includes unexpected pauses, creating a sense of unpredictability in the guitar riff.

Rests in Acoustic Fingerpicking:

Silent Spaces in Fingerpicking Patterns: Utilize silence in acoustic fingerpicking patterns. Brief rests between notes or chords can create a delicate and contemplative atmosphere.

Example: *Dust in the Wind* by Kansas incorporates rests in the fingerpicking pattern, contributing to the song's introspective quality.

Dynamic Release After Silence:

Buildup to Release: Use silence as a buildup to a sudden release of energy, such as a powerful strum or chord. This technique enhances the impact of the release.

Example: John Mayer's *Stop This Train* features a pause before a passionate chord strum, emphasizing the emotional release.

Considerations:

Precision in Timing: Ensure that the timing of the silence is precise to maintain the intended dramatic effect.

Contextual Relevance: Align the use of silence with the context and emotional content of the song.

Experiment with Duration: Vary the duration of pauses to suit the desired impact, ranging from brief rests to more extended silences.

By skillfully incorporating moments of silence or pauses in your guitar compositions, you can create a dynamic and engaging listening experience. Experiment with these techniques to discover how strategic rests can add drama, tension, and emphasis to different sections of your songs.

DYNAMICS AND LYRIC EMPHASIS

If your composition includes lyrics, align dynamic changes with the emotional emphasis of the lyrics. Match intense moments in the lyrics with corresponding dynamic peaks.

ALIGNING DYNAMICS WITH LYRIC EMPHASIS

Aligning dynamics with lyric emphasis is a crucial aspect of crafting a compelling and emotionally resonant song structure in guitar compositions. By carefully coordinating the dynamic elements of your playing with the lyrical content, you can enhance the overall impact and convey the intended emotions more effectively.

Let's explore how to achieve this alignment below.

Understand Lyric Emotion:

Analyze Lyrical Content: Take time to understand the emotional tone and narrative conveyed by the lyrics. Identify key themes, sentiments, and moments that warrant dynamic emphasis.

Example: In Adele's *Someone Like You*, the poignant lyrics about heartbreak and nostalgia align with dynamics that escalate during emotionally charged phrases.

Subtle Dynamics for Introspection:

Soft Dynamics for Introspective Lyrics: During introspective or reflective lyrics, use softer dynamics. This allows the listener to conncct with the vulnerability and depth of the words.

Example: James Taylor's *Fire and Rain* employs gentle dynamics during introspective verses, emphasizing the personal nature of the lyrics.

Dynamic Buildup to Climaxes:

Gradual Dynamics for Building Climaxes: As the lyrics build towards climactic moments, gradually increase the dynamic intensity. This enhances the emotional impact at pivotal points in the song.

Example: Bruce Springsteen's *Born to Run* employs dynamic buildup in the instrumentation to complement the lyrics' themes of escape and freedom.

Powerful Dynamics for Choruses:

Heightened Dynamics for Chorus Impact: Increase dynamics during choruses or sections where the lyrics express heightened emotion or a pivotal message. This adds emphasis and draws attention to the core message.

Example: U2's *With or Without You* features intensified dynamics in the chorus, aligning with the emotional intensity of the lyrics.

Matching Energy Levels:

Align Dynamics with Lyric Energy: Match the energy levels of your guitar playing with the emotional energy conveyed in the lyrics. This ensures coherence between the musical and lyrical components.

Example: The Eagles' *Hotel California* adjusts dynamics to match the varying moods and storytelling within the lyrics.

Dynamic Contrast for Storytelling:

Vary Dynamics to Enhance Storytelling: If the lyrics tell a story with different emotional arcs, use dynamic contrast to underscore these shifts. This helps in creating a dynamic narrative structure.

Example: Johnny Cash's *A Boy Named Sue* utilizes dynamic changes to emphasize the humor and intensity of the story within the lyrics.

Soft Dynamics for Delicate Phrases:

Gentle Dynamics for Delicate Lyrics: When the lyrics contain delicate or sensitive phrases, opt for softer dynamics. This allows for a nuanced and tender expression of the lyrical content.

Example: Nick Drake's *Pink Moon* employs soft dynamics to complement the intimate and introspective nature of the lyrics.

Dynamic Punctuation for Impact:

Use Dynamics to Punctuate Key Phrases: Emphasize important phrases or lines by adjusting dynamics. This adds a sense of punctuation, drawing attention to the lyrical highlights.

Example: Bob Dylan's *Blowin' in the Wind* strategically employs dynamic shifts to accentuate the timeless and impactful lyrics.

Dynamic Response to Emotional Shifts:

Immediate Dynamics for Emotional Shifts: If the lyrics undergo sudden emotional shifts, respond immediately with corresponding dynamic changes.

This enhances the immediacy and authenticity of the emotional expression.

Example: Leonard Cohen's *Hallelujah* adjusts dynamics dynamically to convey the emotional depth of the lyrics.

Dynamic Subtlety in Ballads:

Subtle Dynamics in Ballads: For ballads or slower songs with lyrical depth, incorporate subtle dynamics. This allows the listener to fully immerse themselves in the emotional storytelling.

Example: Eric Clapton's *Tears in Heaven* utilizes gentle dynamics to complement the poignant lyrics about loss and reflection.

Considerations:

Dynamic Control: Develop precise control over your dynamics to ensure a seamless and expressive alignment with the lyrics.

Collaboration with Vocal Dynamics: If working with a vocalist, coordinate dynamics with their vocal delivery to achieve a unified and impactful expression.

Experimentation: Explore various dynamic approaches during the rehearsal process to discover the most effective and emotionally resonant combinations.

By aligning the dynamics of your guitar composition with the lyrical emphasis, you create a cohesive and emotionally resonant musical experience. The synergy between the guitar's dynamics and the lyrics enhances the overall impact of the song, enabling you to effectively convey the intended emotions and narrative.

SWELLS AND FADES

Experiment with swells (gradual increase in volume) and fades (gradual decrease in volume) to shape the overall dynamics of your composition.

EFFECTIVE USE OF SWELLS AND FADES

Using swells and fades is a nuanced technique that can significantly shape the overall dynamics of a song structure in guitar composition. Swells involve gradually increasing the volume, creating a swell of sound, while fades involve a gradual decrease in volume, creating a sense of diminuendo. Employing these techniques adds depth, emotion, and a dynamic ebb and flow to your guitar compositions.

Swells for Intensity Buildup:

Gradual Volume Increase: Use swells to build intensity in a section by gradually increasing the volume of sustained chords or notes. This is effective for creating anticipation and leading into climactic moments.

Example: The Edge in U2's *Where the Streets Have No Name* utilizes swells to build intensity before the song's explosive chorus.

Creating Atmospheric Textures:

Swells for Ambient Soundscapes: Employ swells to create atmospheric textures and ambient soundscapes. This is especially effective in intros, bridges, or interludes where a lush and expansive sound is desired.

Example: Explosions in the Sky, known for instrumental compositions, often uses swells to create ethereal and atmospheric guitar soundscapes.

Fading In for Smooth Transitions:

Fade-In Technique: Start a section with a fade-in to smoothly introduce the guitar part. This technique is particularly useful when transitioning from a quiet to a louder section.

Example: Pink Floyd's *Shine On You Crazy Diamond* features a gradual fade-in, introducing the listener to the ambient guitar textures.

Building Emotional Crescendos:

Swells for Emotional Crescendos: Use swells to build emotional crescendos during climactic moments in the song. This adds a sense of drama and heightens the emotional impact.

Example: The swells in the guitar solo of David Gilmour's *Comfortably Numb* contribute to the emotional intensity of the solo.

Fading Out for Subtle Endings:

Subtle Fade-Outs: Apply a gentle fade-out to conclude a section or the entire song. This is effective for creating a subtle and gradual ending, leaving a lingering impression.

Example: Dire Straits' *Romeo and Juliet* concludes with a gentle fade-out, contributing to the wistful and reflective atmosphere.

Expressive Lead Lines:

Swells with Lead Lines: Introduce expressive lead lines with swells to enhance their impact. This technique works well for adding emphasis to melodic phrases.

Example: Steve Lukather's guitar solo in Toto's *Rosanna* features swells, accentuating the emotive nature of the lead guitar.

Fade-Outs for Ethereal Endings:

Ethereal Endings with Fades: Apply gradual fades for an ethereal ending, allowing the sound to dissipate slowly. This technique is effective for creating a dreamy or contemplative atmosphere.

Example: Radiohead's *Street Spirit (Fade Out)* concludes with a fade-out, contributing to the haunting and ethereal quality of the song.

Transitioning Between Sections:

Swells to Transition: Use swells to transition between different sections of the song. This can smooth out the shifts in dynamics and maintain a seamless flow.

Example: The transition between verses and choruses in Coldplay's *Fix You* is marked by swells, enhancing the overall dynamic structure.

Controlling Feedback with Fades:

Fade to Control Feedback: When using high gain or distortion, employ a gradual fade-out to control feedback and create a controlled decay.

Example: Jimi Hendrix's live performances often featured strategic fades to manage the feedback generated by his high-energy guitar playing.

Adding Dimension to Chord Progressions:

Swells for Chord Progression Dimension: Apply swells to chord progressions to add dimension and a sense of movement. This is effective for creating dynamic interest within repetitive chord sequences.

Example: The swells in Explosions in the Sky's *Your Hand in Mine* contribute to the evolving and dynamic nature of the instrumental piece.

Considerations:

Controlled Technique: Ensure precise control over your volume and technique to execute swells and fades with accuracy.

Use of Dynamics Pedals: Experiment with volume or dynamics pedals to achieve smooth and controlled swells and fades.

Contextual Relevance: Align the use of swells and fades with the emotional context and narrative of the song.

By incorporating swells and fades into your guitar compositions, you can add a layer of expressiveness and dynamic richness. Experiment with these techniques to enhance the emotional impact of your playing and shape the overall dynamics of your song structure.

TONE CHANGES

Note how dynamic changes impact the tone of your guitar. Changes in volume can also influence the timbre and character of your instrument.

BEING MINDFUL OF TONAL CHANGES

Dynamic changes play a crucial role in shaping the tone of guitars in composition. Dynamics refer to variations in volume, intensity, and expression in your playing. These changes have a profound impact on the overall character and emotional depth of the guitar's tone.

Expressive Range:

Soft to Loud Transitions: Dynamic changes allow you to transition from soft, delicate playing to powerful and intense strumming or picking. This expressive range contributes to the emotional depth and versatility of the guitar's tone.

Example: The transition from gentle fingerpicking to powerful strumming in songs like *Blackbird* by The Beatles showcases the expressive range of dynamics.

Tonal Variation with Pick Attack:

Pick Attack Influence: Dynamics affect the way the pick strikes the strings. A gentle pick attack results in a softer, warmer tone, while a more aggressive attack produces a brighter, sharper sound.

Example: Eric Clapton's *Layla* features varying pick attacks, contributing to the tonal variety in the iconic guitar riff.

Sustain and Decay:

Dynamic Impact on Sustain: Playing dynamics influence the sustain and decay of notes. Soft dynamics may create a shorter sustain, while louder dynamics can extend the duration of sustained notes.

Example: The sustained notes in the guitar solo of Pink Floyd's *Comfortably Numb* are shaped by dynamic variations, enhancing the emotional impact.

Volume Swells for Atmosphere:

Swells for Ambient Tones: Using volume swells creates a gradual increase in volume, producing a swelling, atmospheric effect. This technique is effective for creating ambient tones and textures.

Example: The Edge from U2 employs volume swells in songs like *With or Without You* to contribute to the ethereal and atmospheric soundscapes.

Dynamics in Fingerstyle Technique:

Fingerstyle Dynamics: In fingerstyle playing, dynamics are crucial for achieving tonal nuances. Varying the pressure on the strings and the intensity of fingerpicking influences the guitar's tone.

Example: The fingerstyle playing in *Classical Gas* by Mason Williams demonstrates how dynamic control enhances the clarity and expressiveness of each note.

Clean vs. Distorted Dynamics:

Impact on Distorted Tones: Dynamics have a pronounced effect on distorted guitar tones. Soft dynamics may result in a clean or lightly distorted sound, while aggressive dynamics lead to more saturated and overdriven tones.

Example: The dynamic shifts in Metallica's *Enter Sandman* contribute to the alternation between clean verses and heavy, distorted choruses.

Controlled Articulation:

Dynamic Articulation: Dynamics play a role in articulating notes and phrases. Soft dynamics can create a smooth and legato articulation, while harder dynamics produce a more pronounced and staccato effect.

Example: Jazz guitarists often use dynamic articulation to convey nuanced phrasing, as seen in Wes Montgomery's playing.

Accentuating Melodic Phrases:

Dynamics for Melodic Emphasis: Use dynamics to emphasize melodic phrases within a composition. By varying the volume, you can draw attention to specific notes or passages.

Example: In Santana's *Europa*, dynamic changes accentuate the expressive and melodic elements of the guitar solo.

Dynamic Interaction with Effects:

Effects Sensitivity: Dynamics interact with effects pedals. For instance, the response of a distortion pedal can vary based on your playing dynamics, leading to a wide spectrum of tones.

Example: Jimi Hendrix's use of a wah-wah pedal in *Voodoo Child (Slight Return)* responds dynamically to his playing, creating a distinctive and expressive tone.

Dynamic Contrast in Song Structure:

Structural Impact: Dynamic changes contribute to the structural dynamics of a song. Alternating between quiet and loud sections enhances the overall shape and impact of the composition.

Example: The dynamic shifts in Led Zeppelin's Stairway to Heaven contribute to the epic and dynamic journey of the song.

Considerations:

Responsive Playing: Develop a responsive playing technique to effectively control dynamics and bring out the desired tonal qualities.

Contextual Awareness: Consider the emotional context and narrative of the song to determine the most fitting dynamic changes.

Experimentation with Touch: Experiment with variations in touch and finger pressure to explore the tonal possibilities offered by dynamic changes.

Dynamic changes are a fundamental aspect of guitar playing that significantly influence the tone and expressiveness of the instrument. By mastering and strategically implementing dynamic variations in your guitar compositions, you can evoke a wide range of emotions, enhance tonal textures, and bring depth to your musical storytelling.

RECORD AND LISTEN ACTIVELY

Record your composition and listen actively to assess how dynamic changes contribute to the overall impact. Make adjustments based on your observations.

HOW TO LISTEN ACTIVELY TO RECORDINGS

Actively listening to recordings is a key skill for any guitarist aiming to understand and incorporate effective song structures into their compositions. By attentively analyzing existing songs, you can gain insights into arrangement, dynamics, and the overall flow of music.

Focus on the Overall Structure:

Identify Sections: Break down the song into distinct sections like verses, choruses, bridges, and instrumental breaks. Take note of how these sections are arranged and repeated.

Example: In *Hotel California* by Eagles, notice the clear distinction between the verse, chorus, and iconic guitar solos.

Note the Chord Progressions:

Analyze Harmony: Pay attention to the chord progressions used in each section. Understand how chord changes contribute to the emotional shifts and overall feel of the song.

Example: *Wonderwall* by Oasis features a straightforward chord progression that repeats, providing a stable foundation for the song's structure.

Listen to Melodic Elements:

Melodic Hooks: Identify melodic hooks or recurring motifs. These are memorable musical phrases that contribute to the song's identity. Note how they are introduced and repeated.

Example: The guitar riff in Deep Purple's *Smoke on the Water* is a melodic hook that defines the song.

Observe Dynamic Changes:

Dynamic Contrasts: Pay attention to changes in volume and intensity. Note where the dynamics increase or decrease and how this contributes to the overall energy of the song.

Example: The dynamic shifts in Led Zeppelin's *Stairway to Heaven* add drama and impact to different sections.

Study Instrumentation and Arrangement:

Instrumental Layers: Examine the instrumentation and arrangement of the song. Notice how different instruments interact and how the arrangement evolves throughout the track.

Example: The layered instrumentation in Pink Floyd's *Comfortably Numb* creates a rich sonic landscape.

Observe Transitional Elements:

Transitions Between Sections: Pay attention to how the song transitions from one section to another. Identify any transitional elements such as fills, drum fills, or guitar riffs.

Example: The smooth transition between verses and choruses in The Beatles' *Hey Jude* is marked by the repetition of the "na-na-na" vocal line.

Consider Song Dynamics:

Buildups and Releases: Identify moments of buildup and release in the song. Note how tension is created and resolved, contributing to the overall emotional arc.

Example: Radiohead's *Paranoid Android* features dynamic shifts that contribute to the song's unpredictable and dramatic nature.

Examine Lyrics and Themes:

Lyric Structure: If the song has lyrics, examine how they are structured. Identify verses, choruses, and bridges in relation to the lyrical content and themes.

Example: In Bob Dylan's *Blowin' in the Wind*, the straightforward lyric structure complements the song's powerful message.

Notice Production Techniques:

Production Choices: Observe production techniques such as panning, reverb, and effects. These choices can enhance the spatial and atmospheric qualities of the composition.

Example: The use of reverb on The Police's *Every Breath You Take* contributes to the atmospheric and ethereal quality of the song.

Understand Rhythmic Elements:

Rhythmic Patterns: Analyze rhythmic patterns and how they contribute to the overall groove of the song. Identify any variations in rhythm that add interest.

Example: The rhythmic complexity in Fleetwood Mac's *Go Your Own Way* contributes to the energetic feel of the song.

Consider Song Length:

Length and Repetition: Note the overall length of the song and how repetition is used. Identify whether the song follows a traditional structure or if it deviates from standard conventions.

Example: Progressive rock songs like Yes' *Roundabout* often have longer structures with intricate instrumental sections.

Explore Genre-Specific Conventions:

Genre Expectations: Consider the conventions and expectations of the genre. Different genres may have unique structures, and understanding these conventions can inform your own compositions.

Example: Blues songs often follow a 12-bar structure, as heard in B.B. King's *The Thrill Is Gone*.

Tips for Active Listening:

Repeat Listenings: Listen to the song multiple times to fully grasp its structure and nuances.

Use Headphones: Headphones can provide a more detailed and immersive listening experience.

Take Notes: Write down observations and insights as you listen to help internalize the structure.

Active listening to recordings is an invaluable tool for a guitarist looking to refine their understanding of song structure. By analyzing various songs across genres, you can absorb a diverse range of approaches and use this knowledge to inform and inspire your own guitar compositions.

CONSIDERING AUDIENCE EXPERIENCE

Put yourself in the shoes of the listener. Consider how dynamic changes enhance the overall listening experience and emotional engagement.

DYNAMICS AND AUDIENCE EXPERIENCE

When considering how dynamic changes enhance the overall listening experience and emotional engagement of your audience in structuring your song for guitar composition, it's important to ask yourself a series of thoughtful questions. These questions will guide you in crafting a dynamic and emotionally resonant musical journey.

How Can Dynamics Contribute to the Narrative of My Song?

Consider the storyline or emotional narrative of your song. Ask how dynamic changes can reflect and enhance the different phases or emotions within your composition.

What Emotional Impact Do I Want to Achieve in Each Section?

Identify the emotional content you aim to convey in each section of your song. Ask how dynamic shifts can accentuate and intensify the desired emotions.

Where Are the Climactic Moments in My Song, and How Can Dynamics Emphasize Them?

Locate the climactic points in your composition. Explore how dynamic changes leading up to these moments can create anticipation and maximize their impact.

How Can Soft Dynamics Create Intimacy and Draw the Listener In?

Reflect on moments where soft dynamics can create intimacy and draw the listener into the subtleties of your playing. Consider how this contrasts with louder sections.

Are There Opportunities for Sudden Dynamic Surprises to Capture Attention?

Explore the potential for unexpected dynamic shifts. Consider how surprising the listener with sudden changes can add intrigue and captivate their attention.

Do I Have a Gradual Buildup to Create a Climax, and How Can Dynamics Play a Role?

Evaluate whether you have gradual buildup sections leading to climaxes. Determine how dynamics can be strategically employed to intensify the buildup and enhance the climax.

How Can Dynamics Support the Ebb and Flow of Energy Throughout the Song?

Envision the overall energy flow of your song. Ask how dynamic changes can contribute to the ebb and flow, ensuring a dynamic and engaging listening experience.

Where Can I Incorporate Subtle Dynamic Nuances to Add Texture?

Look for opportunities to insert subtle dynamic nuances. Consider how these delicate shifts can add texture and complexity to your guitar composition.

Are Dynamic Changes Consistent With the Mood and Lyrics of Each Section?

Ensure that dynamic changes align with the mood and lyrical content of each section. Assess whether the dynamics reinforce the intended emotional message.

How Can Dynamics Be Utilized to Guide the Listener Through Transitions?

Consider the transitions between sections. Explore how dynamics can act as guiding elements, leading the listener seamlessly from one part of the song to another.

Do I Have Moments of Dynamic Relief to Create Contrast?

Integrate moments of dynamic relief where the intensity subsides. Ask how these quieter intervals contribute to overall contrast and emotional diversity.

Can I Experiment With Unconventional Dynamic Choices to Spark Interest?

Encourage experimentation with unconventional dynamic choices. Explore how unexpected shifts or unique dynamics can add an element of surprise and intrigue.

Am I Utilizing Dynamics to Showcase the Full Range of My Guitar's Tonal Palette?

Consider how dynamics can showcase the full tonal palette of your guitar. Explore the instrument's range from soft and warm tones to bold and bright timbres.

How Can Dynamic Changes Align With Instrumentation and Other Musical Elements?

Ensure that dynamic changes align harmoniously with other musical elements, including vocals and additional instruments. Ask how they can complement and enhance the overall sonic landscape.

Is There a Cohesive Dynamic Arc Across the Entire Song?

Step back and assess the dynamic arc of your entire composition. Ensure that there is a cohesive journey, with dynamics contributing to the overall emotional and musical narrative.

By addressing these questions, you'll gain insights into how dynamic changes can be strategically employed to elevate your guitar composition. Whether aiming for emotional resonance, building tension, or surprising the listener, thoughtful consideration of dynamics enhances the overall listening experience and emotional engagement of your audience.

FEEDBACK

Share your composition with others and seek feedback on the effectiveness of dynamic changes. External perspectives can provide valuable insights.

Sharing Your Composition

When seeking feedback on the effectiveness of dynamic changes in your guitar composition, it's essential to ask targeted questions to gather valuable insights. Constructive feedback can provide you with a fresh perspective and help refine your approach to dynamics.

How Did the Dynamic Changes Impact Your Overall Listening Experience?

Encourage the listener to reflect on how the dynamic shifts influenced their overall experience. This question can help you gauge the emotional impact of your dynamics.

Were the Dynamic Changes Appropriate for the Mood and Emotion I Was Trying to Convey?

Seek feedback on the alignment between your intended mood or emotion and the dynamic changes. Assess whether the dynamics effectively complemented the emotional content of your composition.

Which Sections Benefited the Most From Dynamic Contrasts?

Identify specific sections where dynamic changes stood out positively. This question can help pinpoint areas where your use of dynamics was particularly effective.

Were There Any Moments Where the Dynamics Felt Disjointed or Inconsistent?

Inquire about the overall coherence of your dynamic transitions. Identify any instances where dynamics may have felt abrupt or inconsistent with the flow of the song.

Did the Dynamics Enhance the Buildup to Climactic Moments?

Assess whether the dynamic changes effectively built anticipation and contributed to the impact of climactic moments. This question can reveal the success of your buildup strategies.

Were the Soft Dynamics Engaging and Did They Draw You Into the Music?

Explore how well soft dynamics created a sense of intimacy and drew the listener into the subtleties of your playing. Assess whether softer moments were engaging.

Did You Notice Any Unexpected or Surprising Dynamic Choices?

Inquire about the listener's reaction to unexpected dynamic shifts. Identify whether any surprising choices added interest or if they were perceived as out of place.

How Would You Describe the Overall Dynamic Flow Throughout the Song?

Encourage the listener to provide an overall description of the dynamic flow. This question can reveal patterns, trends, or areas where adjustments might be beneficial.

Were There Moments Where You Felt the Dynamics Could Be More Pronounced or Subtle?

Seek feedback on the range of your dynamics. Determine whether listeners feel certain moments could benefit from more pronounced shifts or subtler variations.

Did the Dynamics Complement Other Musical Elements, Including Vocals or Additional Instruments?

Evaluate how well the dynamic changes aligned with vocals and other instruments. Assess whether the dynamics contributed positively to the overall musical cohesion.

Were There Sections Where the Dynamic Changes Could Be Smoother in Transition?

Inquire about the smoothness of transitions between dynamic changes. Identify any sections where transitions could be improved for a more seamless listening experience.

Did You Feel Engaged Throughout the Entire Song, or Were There Moments of Disinterest?

Explore whether the dynamics maintained listener engagement throughout the entire composition. Identify any moments where interest waned or was sustained.

Were the Dynamics Instrumentally Showcasing the Full Range of the Guitar's Tonal Possibilities?

Ask if the dynamics effectively showcased the diverse tonal palette of the guitar. Determine whether the full range of the instrument's capabilities was utilized.

How Would You Describe the Emotional Arc Created by the Dynamic Changes?

Seek feedback on the emotional journey crafted by your dynamic changes. Understand how listeners perceived the emotional arc throughout the song.

Any Suggestions for Improving the Use of Dynamics in Future Compositions?

Open the floor for constructive suggestions. Encourage listeners to provide insights on how you can enhance your use of dynamics in future compositions.

Tips for Seeking Feedback:

Be Open-Minded: Approach feedback with an open mind, valuing diverse perspectives.

Provide Context: Briefly explain your intentions with dynamics to offer context for feedback.

Encourage Specifics: Ask for specific examples or moments that stood out to the listener.

By posing these questions, you can gather valuable feedback on the effectiveness of dynamic changes in your guitar composition. This input will guide you in refining your approach and further developing your skills in crafting engaging and emotionally resonant musical experiences.

INTENSITY AND RESTRAINT

Find a balance between moments of intensity and restraint. This ebb and flow of dynamics can create a more captivating and dynamic musical journey.

Remember, dynamic changes are not only about volume but also about the emotional impact and expressiveness of your playing. By thoughtfully planning and implementing dynamic shifts, you can elevate your guitar.

BALANCE INTENSITY AND RESTRAINT

Finding a balance between moments of intensity and restraint is a crucial aspect of creating dynamic and engaging song structures in guitar composition. This delicate equilibrium enhances the emotional impact of your music, providing a diverse and captivating listening experience.

Understand the Emotional Context:

Identify Emotional Peaks and Valleys: Consider the emotional journey you want to convey. Determine where intensity is needed for climactic moments and where restraint can create emotional depth.

Map Out the Song's Energy Flow:

Visualize Energy Peaks and Valleys: Imagine the energy of your song as a waveform. Identify sections where you want peaks of intensity and valleys of restraint. This visualization can guide your dynamic choices.

Start with a Strong Foundation:

Establish a Solid Groove or Foundation: Build a strong foundation in sections where intensity is desired. This could be a powerful rhythm, a dynamic chord progression, or a compelling melody that sets the stage for intensity.

Use Dynamic Buildups:

Gradual Intensity Increase: Employ dynamic buildups to escalate intensity gradually. This could involve increasing strumming vigor, introducing additional instrumentation, or elevating the complexity of the arrangement.

Contrast Intense Sections with Moments of Restraint:

Create Breathing Spaces: Counterbalance intense sections with moments of restraint. Provide the listener with breathing spaces where the music pulls back, allowing for emotional contrast and anticipation.

Explore Different Intensity Levels:

Vary Degrees of Intensity: Experiment with different levels of intensity. Not every intense moment needs to be at the highest level; varying intensity levels adds nuance and keeps the listener engaged.

Utilize Articulation Techniques:

Dynamic Articulation: Use articulation techniques like staccato, legato, or slides to control the attack and release of notes. This adds expressiveness and contributes to the ebb and flow of intensity.

Experiment with Timbral Changes:

Timbral Dynamics: Explore changes in tone and timbre. This could involve switching between clean and distorted tones, utilizing different pickups, or applying effects to enhance the sonic variety.

Consider Spatial Dynamics:

Spatial Variation in Dynamics: Experiment with spatial dynamics, such as panning and stereo effects. Shifting the spatial placement of elements can contribute to the perceived intensity or restraint in different sections.

Incorporate Dynamics Pedals:

Use of Volume or Dynamics Pedals: Consider incorporating volume or dynamics pedals to have real-time control over the guitar's intensity. This allows for smooth transitions and dynamic responsiveness.

Create Intense Melodic Climaxes:

Build to Melodic Climaxes: Build intensity around melodic climaxes. This could involve crafting powerful guitar solos, intricate lead lines, or emotionally charged vocal sections.

Silence as a Powerful Tool:

Strategic Use of Silence: Silence is a potent form of restraint. Integrate moments of silence or pauses to create suspense and emphasize key points in your composition.

Maintain a Cohesive Flow:

Cohesiveness Between Sections: Ensure that transitions between intense and restrained sections are smooth. Maintain a cohesive flow so that the shifts in dynamics feel natural rather than abrupt.

Consider Lyrics and Vocal Dynamics:

Align Dynamics with Vocals: If your composition includes vocals, ensure that the dynamics align with the lyrical content. Vocal delivery can significantly impact the perceived intensity or restraint of a section.

Feedback and Iteration:

Seek Feedback on Balance: Share your composition with others and ask for feedback specifically on the balance between intensity and restraint. Use this input for iterative improvements.

Dynamic Structure Mapping:

Create a Dynamic Structure Map: Develop a dynamic structure map that outlines where intensity and restraint are located throughout the song. This visual aid can assist in maintaining balance.

Consider Genre Expectations:

Genre-Specific Considerations: Be mindful of genre expectations. Certain genres may have established conventions regarding when and how intensity and restraint are employed.

Reflect on Overall Song Structure:

Holistic Reflection: Step back and reflect on the overall song structure. Ensure that the balance between intensity and restraint serves the overarching narrative or emotional arc of the composition.

Dynamic Contrast Within Sections:

Micro-Dynamics Within Sections: Introduce micro-dynamics within sections. This involves subtle variations in intensity within a particular part, adding depth without necessarily changing the overall section's character.

Develop a Sensitivity to Context:

Contextual Awareness: Develop a sensitivity to the contextual needs of each section. Consider how the role of your guitar changes based on the context within the song.

Tips for Achieving Balance:

Iterative Process: Achieving the right balance may require multiple iterations. Be patient and open to making adjustments.

Record and Analyze: Record your compositions and analyze them objectively. Listening back can provide valuable insights into the effectiveness of your dynamic choices.

By conscientiously considering these elements, you can strike a balance between moments of intensity and restraint in your guitar composition's dynamics. This balance enhances the emotional resonance of your music

CLOSING

In concluding *Musical Architecture Secrets: Structure Planning For Guitar Composition*, we have embarked on a transformative journey through the intricate world of structure planning, uncovering the essential principles and techniques that lie at the heart of crafting captivating and cohesive musical compositions on the guitar. From the initial spark of inspiration to the final polish, we have explored every facet of the creative process, empowering you to unlock the hidden mysteries behind creating compositions that resonate deeply with your audience.

Throughout our exploration, we have emphasized the importance of **Clarifying Your Vision** as the foundational step in the composition process. By articulating your artistic goals and defining the emotional landscape of your compositions, you have gained clarity and direction in your creative endeavors.

We have delved into the intricate relationship between **Inspiration and Structure**, discovering how to channel creative energy into coherent musical forms that captivate and engage listeners. Through exercises and reflection, you have learned to draw inspiration from diverse sources and infuse your compositions with meaning and depth.

Guided by your innate **Intuition and Structure**, you have navigated the creative process with confidence and conviction, making bold artistic choices and crafting compositions that resonate authentically with your audience. By trusting your instincts and embracing experimentation, you have unleashed your full creative potential as a composer.

Central to our exploration has been the art of **Structure Planning** itself. From analyzing **Common Song Structures** to exploring specialized forms such as **Modal or Freeform Structures** and **Riff-Based Structures**, you have gained a comprehensive understanding of the architectural blueprints that underpin successful compositions.

We have also delved into the intricate details of composition, exploring topics ranging from **Mood and Dynamics** to **Instrumentation and Structure**, **Transitions and Section Lengths**, and **Playing Style and Structure**. Armed with practical tools and strategies, you have honed your compositional skills and learned to sculpt your compositions with precision and finesse.

As we bring our journey to a close, remember that the process of composition is a continuous evolution. Embrace **Revision and Structure** as a natural part of the creative process, and never be afraid to iterate, refine, and improve upon your work. Seek **Feedback** from trusted mentors and peers, and approach each composition as an opportunity for growth and exploration.

In the end, remember that the true measure of a composition lies not only in its technical proficiency but also in its ability to evoke emotion and connect with the listener on a profound level. As you continue on your musical journey, may you always strive for **Intensity and Restraint**, balancing dynamic expression with thoughtful restraint to create compositions that leave a lasting impression on both performer and audience alike.

Thank you for joining me on this enriching exploration of musical architecture. May your compositions continue to inspire and delight, and may you always find joy and fulfillment in the creative process. Keep creating, keep exploring, and above all, keep making beautiful music.

THANK YOU for purchasing *Musical Architecture Secrets: Structure Planning For Guitar Composition* by University Scholastic Press. If you liked this book, please consider spreading your good word!

University Scholastic Press is an internationally renowned publisher and press, writing and producing textbooks, study guides, quote books, workbooks, cookbooks, journals, planners and creative nonfiction novels.

With offices in New York, London and Rome, University Scholastic Press is the trusted leader in producing and writing classic, bestselling books with an original, polished spin.

Other Musician's Series Books
By University Scholastic Press:

A Guitarist's Grimoire: Unlocking the Secrets of Creating A Musical Diary To Master Guitar Composition

Storytelling With Sound: Fundamentals of Creative Guitar Composition

Musical Architecture Secrets: Structure Planning For Guitar Composition

Strings Of Brilliance: Mastering Melody and Harmony Development For Guitar Composition

Rhythm Mastery for Guitarists: Unlocking Tempo and Timing Techniques For Guitar Composition

Index

A

AABA Structure 89
ABAB Structure 93
Analyze Other Musicians 17
Articulation Techniques 177
Audience Attention And Length 138

B

Blend Structures 44
Building Confidence 143

C

Chorus Impact And Length 101
Clarify Your Vision 13
Closing 233
Common Song Structures 31
Consideration of Length 77
Considering Audience Experience 219
Contrast Between Instruments 186
Contrasts And Structure 164
Conventions and Structure 81
Creating Contrast Within Sections 168
Crescendos And Decrescendos 173

D

Determine Section Lengths 77
Dynamic Blueprint Outline 156
Dynamic Contrast And Section Length 122
Dynamics And Lyric Emphasis 202
Dynamics And Melodic Phrasing 182
Dynamics and Section Length 105
Dynamics And Song Structure 148

E

Effective Use Of Swells And Fades 206
Energy Levels And Section Length 113
Exploring Genre-Based Structures 38

F

Feedback 223

Index

G

Genre Structures 38
Gradual Buildups And Structure 160

H

How To Listen Actively To Recordings 214
Hybrid Structures 44

I

Inspiration And Structure 17
Instrumental Sections And Length 130
Instrumental Techniques And Dynamics 190
Instrumentation And Structure 60
Intensity And Restraint 227
Introduction 9
Intuition And Structure 22

L

Lyric And Melodic Content 109

M

Mapping Out Song Structure 27
Modal or Freeform Structures 48
Mood and Dynamics 34
Muted Strums And Picking Patterns 194

N

Narrative Arc 56

O

Other Musician Series Books 237
Other Musician Series Books By
University Scholastic Press 3

P

Playing Style And Structure 68

R

Record And Listen Actively 214
Repetition And Section Length 126
Revision And Structure 73
Riff-Based Structure 52

S

Section Lengths 97
Silence And Pauses 198
Song Narrative And Section Length 118
Structure Planning 27
Swells And Fades 206

T

The Dynamic Blueprint 152
Tone Changes 210
Transitions And Section Length 134
Transitions And Structure 64

V

Verse-Chorus Structure 85